When You're Smiling

When You're Smiling

The Illustrated Biography of

Les Dawson
Foreword by Tracy Dawson

Mick Middles

First published in Great Britain in 1999 by
Chameleon Books
an imprint of André Deutsch Ltd
76 Dean Street
London W1V 5HA

Author's dedication
For Maris

André Deutsch Ltd is a subsidiary of **VCI plc**

www.vci.co.uk

Copyright © **Essential Books 1999**

Design: **Neal Townsend** for **Essential**
Picture research: **Odile Schmitz** for **Essential**

The right of Michael Middlehurst to be identified as the author of this work has been asserted by him in accordance with the Copyright, Designs and Patents Act 1988

1 3 5 7 9 10 8 6 4 2

All rights reserved. This book is sold subject to the condition that it may not be reproduced, stored in a retrieval system, or transmitted, in any form or by any means, electronic, mechanical, photocopying, recording or otherwise, without the publisher's prior consent.

Reprographics by Digicol Link, London
Printed in Italy by Officine Grafiche De Agostini Spa

A catalogue record for this book is available from the British Library

ISBN 0 233 99668 0

Foreword by Tracy Dawson

What a great honour to be able to say a few words about my late, great husband. We were together for seven years and shared some wonderful times, the highlight being the birth of our daughter Charlotte Emily Lesley Dawson on 3 October 1992. She is his legacy and the two of us feel very proud and privileged to bear his surname. It is a great honour, also, that we are invited to attend functions and events which contribute to keeping his name going. The marvellous thing about Les is that everyone has a kind word to say about him and he is remembered with such love and affection. A true comedian's comedian, all his fellow comics agree that his humour was the best. It's wonderful that it lives on through television and is still on daily, while the many books he wrote are a testament to his literary skills. I feel it a privilege to have known and loved him and feel certain he will never be forgotten by any of us.

Introduction

A MATE OF MINE, WELL, NOT A MATE EXACTLY, JUST THIS GUY WHO WOULD STAND AT THE BAR AT ONE OF MY OLD LOCAL PUBS, USED TO TELL ME A STORY ABOUT LES DAWSON.

He said that he was standing there, drinking, one evening, when in walked Les. Completely out of the blue. They sank into a drunken huddle of camaraderie. He said that Les poured his heart out that night, told him things he could never repeat, lest some tabloid ears picked up on the story. He added that they finished the evening by staggering out of the pub, arm in arm and, ever since that day, twenty years ago, Dawson never dropped him from his Christmas card list… and telephoned two or three times a year.

The story isn't true. Well, it could be true but, as my acquaintance was a blabbering idiot full of such stories, I can't really see it. But I always thought it interesting that he perceived Les Dawson to be some kind of soul-mate. You couldn't imagine spending such an evening with Bernard Manning, could you? Or Frank Carson. Or Ken Dodd, who is a phenomenon totally beyond the scope of my understanding. But Les Dawson… Oh, I wish he'd walked into my pub.

I don't possess a unique talent. I cannot fill this book with exquisitely daft and surreal one-liners. I cannot pour my miserable self onto a page in such a way. I cannot hide a deep solemnity behind a humour so powerful it affects everyone it touches. I just cannot move people like that. I cannot even imagine what it must be like to be able to reduce people to that blubbery state where uncontrollable laughter is checked by a tear in the eye. That doesn't bother me. Few people can, and perhaps nobody could do it as well as Les Dawson, the most fascinating British comedian in recent memory.

Les Dawson. His face conveyed complete sardonic resignation

When You're Smiling

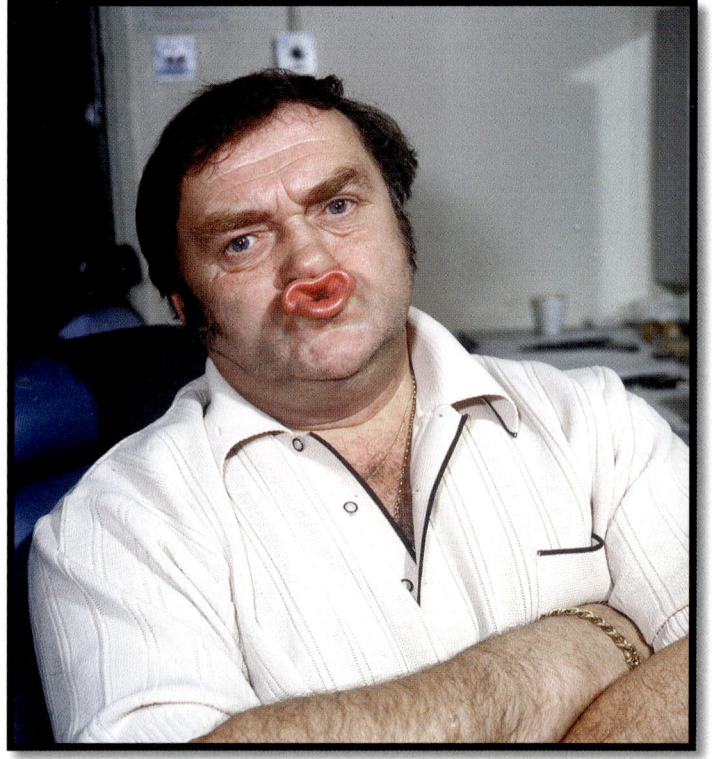

Lips that would kiss…

I was sitting in the ostentatious Victoria and Albert Hotel, in Manchester's Castlefield district, literally yards away from the austere *Coronation Street* set. The place was filled with glittery and vivacious starlets from that very soap, all squealing and chortling with a rather disappointingly bland selection of local footballers, dull lads with streaked hair, dangling Ferrari keys. But none of these had anything to do with my name-drop.

I was sitting on a sofa, pouring coffee for one of the most instantly recognisable faces in Britain. It was a golden moment, because I'm convinced that he was genuinely determined not to succumb to the shallow glamour sparkling away mere feet from our table. And all the lovely starlets were glancing in his direction. *Coronation Street* girlies nodded in hopeful acknowledgement and Kevin Kennedy – Curly Watts – smiled directly

Introduction

at him. But my guest, one of the nicest men I have ever met, showed no interest whatsoever in such sycophancy. He was talking to me, Godammit! Our interview, scheduled for half an hour, was seeping past 180 minutes and was drifting into a dreamily chummy stage.

My guest was Michael Parkinson and he was talking about the most impressive people he had ever met. Is there anyone else on Earth who has met and perceptively probed a more impressive array of interviewees? The obvious names – Muhammad Ali, George Best, Billy Connolly – fluttered past before his lengthy list got to Les Dawson. I swear a tear crept from his eye. From mine too, though it was probably a sycophantic secretion. 'Les,' he offered, opening out his palms in a gesture of helplessness, 'How can I describe Les? Beyond anything really, Les was Les! Unique! Everybody knows it.'

He drifted into a little day-dream at that point. It could have been about some obscure club cricket match in 1950s Barnsley, or some local footballer called Clogger Bates or something else completely. This was Michael Parkinson and things like that are important in his world. I like to think he was dreaming about that priceless moment when he, the most composed and elegant television interviewer of all time, allowed his composure to evaporate, leaving him a giggly, blubbery huddle unable to ask the next question. He had, he would later admit, met his match.

All his interviewee, Les Dawson, had done, was smile, gurn a bit, and continue smiling. It was so funny. I have no idea why. To be honest, I can't stand gurners. Generally they give me the creeps. I don't go a bundle on northern comics, either. Or working men's clubs. I can't even last for more than five minutes in Les Dawson's beloved Blackpool. Awful place. Give me a Knutsford wine bar, any day. I don't like fish'n'chips. Couldn't eat a pineapple fritter to save me life.

I guess Les Dawson wouldn't have liked me. I'm from glamorous Stockport. I would have been Roy Barraclough's affected Cissie to Dawson's salt o' the Earth Ada. Dawson always favoured the Adas of this world. Fair enough.

I found him funny, though. From the very first time I glanced at his face on *Opportunity Knocks*. And I hated *Opportunity Knocks* too, and Hughie Green, and all the hapless geeks who submitted to his patronising nature. And all the other comics on early 1970s television. Boy, did we watch some crap in those days.

Michael Parkinson was hardly alone in his adoration of this disarming Mancunian. While I was writing this little book, all manner of folk would ask me, 'What are you

When You're Smiling

working on now?' They weren't really interested, to be honest, and I didn't blame them. They had children to scold and plumbers to scream at. I think they expected me to reply with something tedious like, 'Oh, The Stone Roses,' after which their eyes would glaze over and they would hastily retreat into the familiar territory of gossip. However, when I said, 'Oh, Les Dawson,' something rather strange would happen. 'Les Dawson?' they would say, warming instantly to the subject. 'Now that is interesting. I loved Les Dawson, I'll never forget that time…'

You have no idea how many times that has happened. Indeed, I have scoured the country, not just Stockport, but even the mysterious land that lies beyond, and I have yet to meet a single person, preacher or punk, poet or proctologist, who didn't express a remarkable fondness for poor old Les. Did everybody love him? It would seem so. I can think of a worryingly large number of British comedians who have inspired exactly the opposite effect – no names, though I'm sure you can come up with a few yourself – but it is indeed a tiny and fiercely exclusive club who can claim to have connected with the people in the way that Les Dawson could. Whatever Les did, even if it was nothing more than a guest spot on some dreadful revue wrapped around the ego of a cheesy host more deserving a round of machine-gun fire rather than applause – he brought a strange, unpretentious intelligence. He was first and foremost a writer who had perfected the art of the self-deprecating one-liner and had carried it into a whole new area. Through a severe apprenticeship in the weird culture of northern working men's clubs, he built his act around that culture. Perhaps more remarkably, given the often apathetic response from the crowds in his early years, he managed to convey a respect for his audience, even if they only consisted of five comatose fish-gutters in Grimsby. Never patronising. Never pretentious. Never lost in ambition or ego.

He wasn't perfect. There were times when the humour drained from his grumblings and he edged towards the curmudgeonly. But such things were swiftly forgiven. As Michael Parkinson succinctly observed, 'Les was Les.' Everybody knew it. Everyone, even my inebriated friend at the bar, knew he was – as so few entertainers are – for real.

*   *   *

Introduction

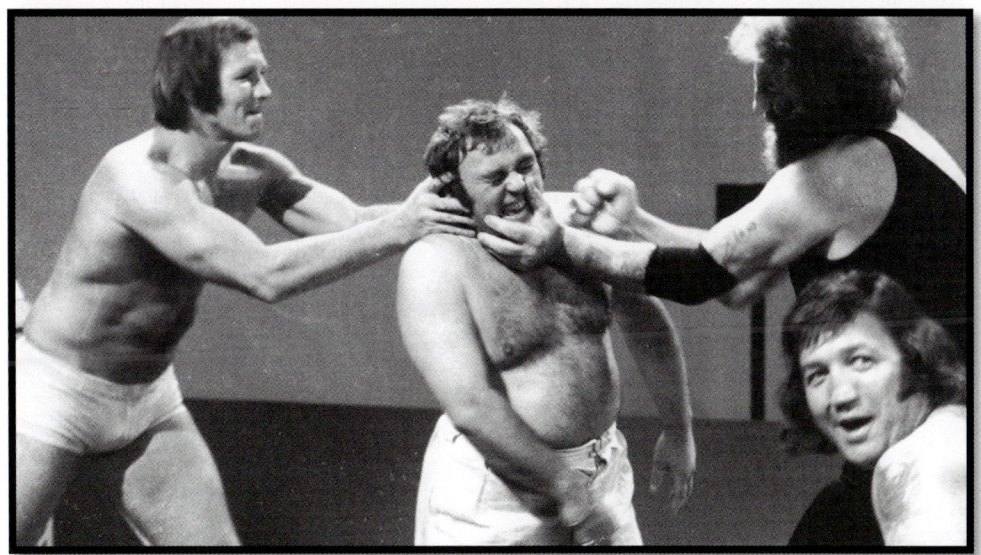

Diversity unparalleled. Wrestling skills to match his piano playing

Chapter One

Canals and Meaning

1931. GRIM BUILDINGS, SOOT-BLACK AND LEERY, CROWDING OVER TEEMING STREETS. MANCHESTER CITY CENTRE, CRAMMED WITH ARCHITECTURAL OSTENTATION. BEAUTIFUL BUILDINGS, TOO…

… somewhere, deep within the grime, within the residue of the distant industrial revolution. Buildings of power, the jewels of perverse wealth, forming a city, forming a commercial heart.

Back in the 1840s, if viewed from the Pennine foothills, Manchester's skyline was one of the most extraordinary sights in the world. That black city centre flanked by a mass of flat-topped, red-bricked factories, stretching gloomily out to a ring of grey towns, from Oldham to Wigan, Stockport to Bolton. A strangely aesthetic sight, its romance caught the attention of Benjamin Disraeli, the novelist prime minister, who stated: 'Manchester is as great a human exploit as Athens.' An interesting choice of words indeed. Was he standing on Werneth Low to the east, squinting at the city through the murk, the smog that hung over Manchester like an umbrella? Or was his little word-play simply hinting at the pain, the killing poverty, the ferocious 'exploitation', of working children, for example, whose hands helped to physically build one of the greatest cities in the world?

Today it isn't difficult to see the beauty of Manchester. The soot has gone, the blackness scraped and blasted away to welcome a softer, gentler time. In the 1990s,

Young Les: King of the Clubs

When You're Smiling

people actually 'look' at these buildings – they flock in, by coach and rail, from Wales, France, China, even, entranced by the city's strange allure.

'By 'eck,' they would 'ave laughed, in the owd days. 'Folk comin' in ter look at our buildings? Pah!' How stupid, how frivolous that notion would have seemed.

Les Dawson was born, in 1931, in this one-time giant of Britain's industry. He was born into slump. Into cloying, life-threatening poverty, daily uncertainties of health. But also into a warm and loving family.

When he was a lad, for young and old alike, architectural beauty remained hidden. It lay in a different world, in the future. In the themed 1990s, when heavy industry lay dead in one giant, prettified museum. Disraeli's aesthetically pleasing Manchester was a distant notion, lost in the daily scrape for survival.

There has been, since then, a shift of evil. Those buildings: the sheer force of money that brought the finest architects in the world into the town, to build warehouses with Grecian colonnades, for the captains of industry to freeze themselves in frock-coated statuary. Marvelled at, today. Sneered at, back in 1937, as you scurried through the town.

And Les Dawson, as a lad, did scurry through Manchester city centre, cowed beneath those buildings, born into submission. For, until the evocative 1960s, the evil of Manchester still lay in that architecture. In recent times, that evil has shifted into the culture of drugs, of guns, of prevailing criminality which, terrifyingly, has seeped into the heart of inner city society. Things are not better today. You cannot destroy an evil – you wipe it out, but it springs up somewhere else.

Les Dawson was born into the old world. His writing, his humour, his art, was powered by the beauty of Manchester. But it wasn't the beauty of the city centre. It was the beauty of the people. People living on the precarious brink of real poverty but fighting back, with a sheer power of human spirit, and with human generosity too. People who could leave their front doors open, allow their children to wander freely, unharmed, among Lowryesque streets, a sign of a social camaraderie that no longer exists.

The ostentatious heart of Manchester was still ringed with a thick, dark collar of poverty. As in Leeds, as in Sheffield, as in London. You could walk into it, from Piccadilly. It would take minutes. All you had to do was saunter along eternally raucous Oldham Street, where musicians and folk bands played to brawling beerheads, where beggars

Canals and Meaning

The fine art of gurning

15

When You're Smiling

A brief glimpse of the tension usually hidden behind the comedic front

lurked, hunched in the alleys, literally with daggers in hand, waiting to pounce. The violence was always there, on the edge of that poverty, but it rarely filtered into local gossip, let alone the local press. It would take a murder, and a particularly inventive murder at that, to tweak the imagination of the local reporters. It is a myth to suggest that violence didn't exist. It did. But it was swept under the mat, like a great deal of other stuff that was grubby and undesirable.

Drift northwards through the vast cotton warehouse land of Ancoats, cross the arterial thoroughfare of Oldham Road, and turn right onto the equally vast Rochdale Road, where a string of squalid houses flanked each pavement, liberally dotted with shops and pubs. A mile of this, and there you were. Thirties Collyhurst. Terraced housing. Line after line after line of houses, a ribbed network of homesteads. Blackened and cobbled. Backyards and alleyways. Pubs on every corner. Grocers, general and green-, peppered the streets. Headscarved housewives chattering over garden walls, drunken husbands staggering back from the pub, and kids everywhere, scrabbling about, scuffling in the grime. Swinging on rope tied to lampposts. Scrapping in the ginnels. Every kid, it seemed, was a scuff-kneed oik. Clean for five minutes and then coated in grime for the remainder of the day, but in and out of every house, in and out of every yard.

Then as now, the women ruled the roost. Their solid pragmatism laid down the rules while the men drifted out each day with faint hope of work. If lucky, they found it, perhaps labouring for a transient builder. If they were very lucky, they returned armed with enough 'brass' to enter the true heart of their kingdom, the men-only tap room, where reality was hung near the door with the coats, and pub games, football and fighting ruled the gossip. Two hours later, into their fourth or fifth pint of bitter, the horrors of the world had vanished. It was a sad cycle.

> Les Dawson: 'Our terraced house was so narrow the mice walked on their back legs and the kitchen ceiling was so low the oven had a foot-level grill.'

Terraced-house life, championed in the 1980s and 1990s after the horrors of high-rise estates and horrific 1970s architectural experiments, wasn't exactly the nirvana mythology claims it was – families warmly gathering around the piano for a good old singsong, a mug of Horlicks, a bottle of stout and cheery family banter. The reality was a

When You're Smiling

rather harsher battle against draughts and cold, family problems and the ever-present threat of illness. It was also, for the Dawsons and most of their neighbours, cramped. Les, his mother Julia, and father, also called Les, his mother's parents, David and Ellen Nolan, and his uncle Tom (everyone had an uncle Tom), all squashed noisily into a two-up, two-down terrace on Thornton Street.

The house was, as Les would often state, 'filled with love'. The kind of unconditional love that, although it still exists in most families today, doesn't spill out into the streets, or permeate into the neighbours' front rooms, in quite the same way. But even that love, a love strong enough to provide unstinting support for Dawson during his early career, wasn't always enough when five adults and one child fought for personal space in a two-bedroomed house. Especially as there were days when the household budget dried up and food became sparse. Even at best, the food of Les Dawson's childhood was basic. Filling. It was ballast, stacked with carbohydrates. No time, really, to think about vitamins and nutrients. To indulge even the mildest food affectation would be regarded, quite rightly, as obscene flippancy. Bread and dripping may sound like a particularly vivid northern cliché today but it was, like potatoes – boiled, chipped or mashed – a way of filling stomachs cheaply and keeping those aching pangs at bay.

Dawson's parents never knew the comforts of security. His dad was hard-working, but building-site labourers could do little more than flit from job to job, hoping for something more permanent, which usually never came. His dad was also an inveterate card-sharp, a street-wise and shifty billiards hustler and a skilful darts player. All things which could generate small amounts of money quickly, although often at some personal risk. These were the 1930s and they would cast a shadow over every single thing that Les Dawson would ever do. Forty years later, seeing a plate of unfinished food, he could mislay his loveable persona and fly into a rage. But that was his heart and, corny as it sounds, it was to prove his most valuable asset.

The Dawsons moved house often and quickly. The phrase 'moonlight flit' is bandied around cheaply nowadays but, in the 1930s and 1940s, escaping the grip of rent men, of all manner of unsalubrious creditors, was a fact of life for many households. Consider this. Late, one dank, misty night, Les's parents bundled all their essential possessions onto a rickety cart and, dragging Les along with them, pushed the ungainly carriage up Rochdale Road for two miles until reaching Moston Lane, and then on into the rather optimistically named New Moston. They were on a flit to a rented flat, incredibly modern

Canals and Meaning

for the 1930s. It was, in truth, just a shunt from one mode of poverty to another. The flat did, however, come complete with a garden. Not a yard, a garden. A real garden. With grass. Little Les, eight years old, lay face down in that grass, smelling it, rippling his fingers through it, digging them into the dirt, flipping over and soaking in the luxury of sunshine – and, yes, even in a poverty-stricken Manchester edging into the Second World War, the sun did occasionally shine. For the first time in his life. A simple but valuable pleasure, as he later explained to Radio Four:

> 'It was an aesthetic experience. My first conscious aesthetic experience. The sun on the grass, the smell, just sitting there, soaking it all in. It was sheer pleasure and there was precious little sheer pleasure around in 1939.'

The joy of this experience would linger in his memory into later life, although it would swiftly fade in the young Dawson's mind. Once again, he succumbed to the cramped surroundings. He made do. Europe was transforming into a war zone and Les Dawson was making do with a bit of grass and a grimy pavement. That was his world.

At Moston Lane Infants' Elementary School, he struggled. Not with the learning process – his intelligence shone through from the beginning. He was never top, but he was forever hovering with intent, especially in English, where his imagination carried him onto a plane rarely visited by the grubby oiks of New Moston. Even at primary school there were signs, all too often quickly repressed, of a fascination with words. He wrote essays and poetry, far better than anyone else in the school. Not that this mattered a jot. Schoolboy kudos was not to be gained by scribbling a few dumb observations in a junior textbook.

To gain credibility, like all kids his age, he grubbed about. In alleyways, on the dour green knolls of Moston Brook, in the curiously downbeat leisure offered by the gloriously named Boggart Hole Clough, a grassy expanse which came complete with its own mythical fantasy creatures. (The 'Boggarts', they were called. Little buggers they were, messing about with people's lives. Dawson loved the idea of these 'bad elves' and, later, even filtered them into his surreal monologues.)

Overleaf: Dinner-suited northern grit

When You're Smiling

The war came to Collyhurst with a vengeance. It was, after all, on the fringe of a blitzed city centre and anyone who believes that inner city life wasn't without serious dangers might note that one day, as the young Les sauntered to school, no doubt dreaming about being a soldier, a German fighter plane zipped down Rochdale Road, machine-gunning – but mercifully missing – a line of kids on the pavement. There were rumours, never proven but still circulating in the local pubs, that German planes had been instructed to drop unspent armoury, bombs or bullets, on the houses to the north of Collyhurst, in Prestwich and Cheetham Hill – then, as now, predominantly Jewish areas.

An unexploded bomb forced Les and his mother into a nearby rest home, while his father served in the desert, in the Eighth Army. At times, the blitz was absolutely deafening, a terrifying ordeal. Rubble-strewn streets with bodies folded into the debris. One night, Les and his friend Ken Cox, somewhat recklessly camping in the Ashworth Valley, had to flee the clutches of two escaped German prisoners of war. But of course, it wasn't all bad times. There was a resurgence of human kindness and undoubtedly this noticeable swell of goodness also had a profound effect on Dawson:

> 'How I yearn to turn the clock back and meander through Ancoats and Miles Platting, then on to Moss Side where the black population's culture has blended with the Irish of Hulme and Greenhays. Despite the ruthless modernisation that has tended to destroy the Manchester I knew, the character of its people keeps alive the crowded friendliness that is the hallmark of the city. Some good things have emerged. The River Irwell is cleaner than it has ever been. I remember it used to be so polluted the fish living in it didn't have fins, they had grease nipples.'
> (From *Les Dawson's Lancashire*).

At the age of twelve, he was moved again. This time to the comparative luxury of 21 Keston Avenue, Higher Blackley. A semi in a cul-de-sac, in the rarefied atmosphere of the spacious dwellings to the south of Victoria Avenue. To Dawson, it 'felt like living in the Albert Hall'.

It is a tradition, and perhaps even a cliché, that comics learned at an early age to escape trouble by telling jokes. With Les Dawson, this scenario was taken a step further. The jokes were there but they came a poor second to his unique talent for 'gurning'.

Canals and Meaning

It wasn't called gurning when Les did it. It wasn't called anything, because no one had ever done it like Les, before. Not in Higher Blackley, anyway. It was extraordinary. To Dawson's amazement, he found that by flipping his face he was able to introduce a curious merriment into even the most tense moments of street aggression. In North Manchester during the Second World War, teenage street violence was never too far away. Les wasn't hugely popular before or during his teens (though of course, the very concept 'teenager' didn't exist in those days) and found it difficult to mix easily. Others found him funny, but it was curiously difficult to regard him as a soul-mate. He was an oddity, drifting around the social fringe of a town blitzed and defiant, burning by night, smoking by day.

There was one school incident which almost certainly boosted his confidence and hinted, weakly, at some kind of distant future which might involve writing. One of Dawson's teachers, Bill Hetherington, stood Les before the whole class, and tore into his lack of application in the areas of maths and geography. Schools were hardly rife with gentle persuasion, and Les was reduced to sobs after six slaps of an extremely hard cane. Afterwards, a curious thing happened. The teacher read a particularly vivid essay from Dawson's text book. The class sat dead still, expecting and probably even hoping for further chastisement. The essay, entitled 'A Winter's Day', was a little wordy, in the manner of a pupil who had suddenly discovered verbs but not how to keep them under control. Nevertheless, it was head and shoulders above the essays by his classmates. Hetherington waited for the class laughter to die away before saying how good the essay was for one so young, and adding that Dawson had 'the talent to be a fine writer'. It was an important moment, one which Les would never forget and for which he would remain forever grateful. It was the first time that anyone had acknowledged that he was talented. Without that boost, he would surely have struggled even more.

* * *

Chapter Two

Searching

PLANNING A **FUTURE** WASN'T DIFFICULT. THE **OPTIONS** WERE **SLIM**.

Respectability, at least in the eyes of the pushier mothers, lay in some kind of job in the retail trade, or pen-pushing in an office. It lay in anything other than basic casual labouring which passed as work for the city's unemployed. Les Dawson's mum presumed that her son would sink quietly, but safely, into a job at the local Co-op, or Kwaaarp!, as it was pronounced. Her aspirations were built from common sense. The Co-op was a proper place, offering proper jobs, often with a pension. Far more respectable than scrapping about for casual work which, in her eyes, too often led to afternoons down the pub. Young Les was bright. He was no genius – or so they thought – but he was destined for more than the hod.

He was just fourteen when he left school, as most boys did then, and dutifully applied for a job at the Co-operative Wholesale Society in Balloon Street. It was situated near Victoria Station and the trade district of Shude Hill and Dantzig Street then, as now, a curious mixture of businesses thriving in spite of a downbeat, seedy atmosphere. Nevertheless, it was a job and, much to the pride of his mother, it was in the drapery department. Returning home each evening and, each Friday, clutching his brown envelope containing one hard-earned guinea, he felt like a conquering hero. He was up and running. There was, however, one incident as seedy as Shude Hill itself, when a fellow male worker attempted to rape the young Les. It was an incident that put paid to any vestiges of naïveté. A weird, secretive incident, too as, in those days, homosexuality was certainly never spoken about in tough North Manchester. Les Dawson cracked his assailant with a crowbar. Other than that, working life was simply dull.

Those Olympian aspirations proved slightly over-ambitious

When You're Smiling

Angelic innocence

It wasn't to last, anyway. When asked to move to a different department, he began to feel unhinged, unwanted. Thus began his weary spell as an apprentice electrician. This was a strange world indeed. A mixture of complex technicalities and ferocious bottom-rung camaraderie. It was an environment alien to him and his meagre standing in the Co-op slipped further and further. He was transferred to the bold and brassy electrician's department, but it became obvious that he just wasn't cut out for the job.

National Service, so often the source of prime comic material, came as a relief to the electrically-challenged Dawson. Freed from the horrors of his apprenticeship, he threw himself into the routine. Dawson was sent to Catterick Camp, which was a heady experience, to put it mildly. Conscripts would arrive at the handsome Yorkshire town of Richmond. This was merely a savage ruse, intended to inject a brief feeling of serenity before the rigours of stark, nearby Catterick dawned in all their horror. Living through a blitz was nothing compared to Catterick.

The traumas, the bonhomie, the savage hierarchy would provide the perfect opportunity for Les to observe the human condition, often under extreme and unnatural pressure. As he would later explain, although, unusually, not in a comic mode, to BBC Radio Four:

> 'During National Service I discovered that feeling that all writers get, actually, perhaps everybody gets. But it was the feeling that you are watching everything happening as if it was a film. That's how I got through the days. Of course it was grim. At times it was unbearable but, if you told yourself that you were just an observer, just researching perhaps, although I didn't know what researching was at the time, it somehow made things easier. It was, let's face it, a really surreal situation to be in, and as such offered limitless comic possibilities. I can't say that I hated it. It didn't make a man of me, or anything like that, but it was an interesting diversion. Things, after all, were pretty grim in post-war Manchester so, in a way, even bunking down in some freezing dorm seemed a little bit exotic.'

In his autobiography, *A Clown Too Many*, Les Dawson recalled the immense feeling of release when, following the first six traumatic weeks as a lowly new recruit, he suddenly felt like a soldier, like a man:

> 'I began to learn the art of surviving in a military jungle. When my kit was stolen I went out and stole someone else's. When any NCO appeared, I made myself look busy. I learned never to volunteer for anything and older hands taught me how to sneak out for an evening's booze in Richmond.'

Put simply, he learned the ropes. Not how to serve his country, exactly, but how to play the game to his own advantage. In Chester and, later, in Germany, he discovered the full absurdities of army life, especially army life in post-war Europe. It was a bizarre, insane continent where the only way to survive was, yet again, to play the game.

When You're Smiling

National Service took two years from Les Dawson. What he gained from the experience, apart from his comic observance, was a sense of distance from working-class Manchester, which could be cloying, even deadening. Through National Service, he met different people, people from rural towns and people from the south. It broadened him. It also gave him a worrying appetite for travel, for the unusual. Far from adding sensible blinkers, National Service created a desire for adventure. Les knew that, upon being demobbed, he would probably resume his dreaded trainee electrician's post at the Co-op, which he duly did, but it would be a short-term measure. Which was just as well, because he was almost instantly sacked: 'quite rightly, in the interests of public safety. I was a menace with that screwdriver, left to my own devices I would have done more damage than the blitz…' he noted dryly.

The aforementioned Uncle Tom quickly provided him with a diversion, encouraging the young Les to try his hand at the noble art of boxing. It was popular pastime back then, especially among those suffering from demob frenzy, and then, as now, offered gifted fighters an escape route out of poverty. For obvious reasons, these potentially wild youths were heartily encouraged into the ring. Dawson wasn't a natural, not like his Uncle who, twenty years earlier, had crafted himself a fearsome reputation as a Collyhurst street-fighter. This was very much something to be in the late 1920s, and not a career one took up lightly. Les had similar skills. He was well-built, broad-shouldered and surprisingly quick. What he lacked, however, to his uncle's chagrin, was any trace of killer instinct. At that time there was an atmosphere inside some venues – Ardwick Lads' Club, in particular, remained in his memory – that took pugilism beyond mere sport. All too often, boxing was seen as legalised street-fighting, rather than a noble art intended to encourage good-hearted competition and mutual respect.

And that was something that, after his National Service stint, Les Dawson was beginning to miss. He toyed briefly with the idea of joining the army, as a possible 'way out'. Young and suddenly fired with possibility, he felt something welling inside him. It was an artistic hunger, something he had all but lost after leaving school.

Dawson flitted from pub to pub at nights, drinking heavily and charming as many girls as possible. But it was a shallow existence overshadowed by depression and a bleak awareness of his lack of options. His parents began to despair.

He started to write, copiously and, many thought, pointlessly. Writing wouldn't put bread on't table, was the general consensus, and it wasn't difficult to see their point.

Searching

Would you buy a Hoover from this man?

When You're Smiling

Writing existed in a fantasy world, some time in the future and most likely in some soft foreign clime. Certainly not in 1940s Manchester, which was something of a shame as it was an exceptionally evocative time. Manchester remained one of the great industrial cities of the world, half-crumbled, half-defeated, but battling back. Still blackened with soot, still dramatic and awe-inspiring. The perfect place to stimulate aesthetic appetites, if not to encourage a Bohemian bent. But that is exactly what Les Dawson desired. He needed – and he kept this to himself lest his manliness be challenged – an artistic escape. He had learned the piano, back in the singalong days of a pre-television childhood, and his bass baritone singing voice was pleasant, if untutored.

Encouraged by his sudden desire to learn, to improve himself, his hand turned to poetry, to short stories, which he excitedly whisked off to various publications. At the time, there was a curious boom in magazines of poetry and fiction, selling to a general public not willing to splash out on books. Dawson perused these magazines with puppy-dog eagerness, his mood darkening only when the rejections duly arrived. No matter – the bug had bitten. Les Dawson had become a writer, if only in his own head. And what did writers do? Simple. They went to Paris, rented a garret, drank enormous amounts of coffee and wine, smoked cigarettes from morning to night and produced a work of such palpable genius that literary superstardom would swiftly beckon.

Dawson managed to accomplish the first few tasks on the list with relative ease. It was just the literary superstardom bit that eluded him. Nevertheless, to up sticks in Higher Blackley and settle so optimistically on the Left Bank was a move that took a considerable amount of courage. His writing output increased, as did his descriptive skills. And the dramatic change of scenery certainly provided the necessary inspiration:

> 'I was trying to write essays. Things like, "Grimy hunched warehouses clutching the skyline with dissipated profiles, gazing eyeless upon litter pitted streets." I never, for one moment, thought that I might have a slight problem making a living out of writing such stuff. I never even thought about who might actually buy this writing. I just thought that you wrote and somehow got paid. Looking back, I must have been so incredibly naïve, I really must. That sort of stuff is about as commercial as trying to be the fiddler on the roof in Iraq. And quite rightly so, because I hadn't worked out that there has to be some point behind descriptive writing. Even if it just used to lead people into a ridiculous joke, as I

did. Then that's fine. But the writing on its own, with no story, with no hook, is just schoolboy stuff, really. It took me a long time to realise that...

'I wandered down Monsieur Le Prince, a small winding street on the Left Bank and I walked into a bar and there was a beautiful piano there. I just sat down and started playing it. It seemed like the natural thing to do. And this Madame came out, dressed completely in red. I thought she was a pillar box. Anyway, she offered me a job playing piano, late nights. It was the best job I ever had because she plied me with cheap red wine, so I was just drunk the entire time. But I couldn't understand the point, because nobody came in at all. Absolutely nobody. People would walk past and go in the back, but they would never linger in the bar. I thought it was my playing that put them off but the Madame was really pleased. The thing was that the bar area was just the front for a brothel. She didn't want me to entertain the customers at all, just to provide a slight diversion at the entrance. But it was still a great job.'

In Paris, Dawson's piano-playing lifted him slightly above the poverty line. It wasn't enough. His writing slowed to a halt, as his piano-playing took up more and more time. It was during this spell that he accidentally found a new direction. Tired of being so studiously ignored by people who had heard more of his piano-playing than was healthy, Dawson started to create his own ear-catching style. Initially using jazz notes, he invented what would later become his celebrated trick of performing off-key, in a parallel, tune-crunching universe. To his delight, he caught the attention of the people drifting in and out of the brothel. Word of mouth even provided him with a small, inebriated following. The pay was, alas, too little to allow him anything more than the Parisian basics which, disappointingly, were exactly the same as Mancunian basics but with garlic.

After four hard but illuminating months, Dawson was back in Blackley for a period of reassessment and a little wound-licking. He consoled himself by accepting that he had, at least, discovered some kind of direction. Using his communication skills, he briefly took up the job of selling insurance. This wasn't the lucrative career it is today. It was very much a bicycle-clips-and-club-money existence, peddling tiny policies. Once again, he faced the sack and, of course, there was a certain amount of stigma attached to that.

When You're Smiling

Neighbourhood gossips would hunch over garden fences, circulating vengeful tittle tattle: 'He will never settle down, that one.' Perhaps they were right.

Dawson's next job, playing piano in a local pub, paid him the princely amount of ten bob for a three-hour stint. Not at all bad, but it hardly seemed a sensible or lasting career move. For Dawson, though, it proved a tremendous breakthrough. It was the bottom rung, but he had made a start in showbiz. He was Les Dawson, musician and entertainer. It sounded grand. The reality was so absurdly down to Earth that he had to approach his task with a sense of humour.

This was to become a crucial period in Dawson's showbiz apprenticeship. It was a period where, with absolutely no encouragement, he started to create his own surreal world, combining his musicianship with a wild flux of ideas. Moreover, they were ideas that nobody could comprehend. Artistically, Les Dawson was living entirely in his own world. It would eventually become the making of him, although for many years it provided him with little more than ridicule.

Musicians? He was a musician, was he? He didn't know whether he was any good or not, but his attention had been grabbed by the jazz music that had swept into the city along with the American servicemen, still stationed in Warrington and Ashton-Under-Lyne, bringing a whole new concept – glamour – to Manchester's dour streets. By the start of the 1950s, jazz was a big deal in Manchester. Swing bands settled into the basements of large department stores and the large Victorian pubs of Oldham Street and Piccadilly were suddenly enlivened by jazz. It was a pre-rock 'n' roll Americanisation. Les Dawson wanted in and joined Manchester's Cotton Pickers' Jazz Band. He wasn't paid a thing, but at least, and at last, he had fallen in with a group of lively, artistic minds.

*   *   *

Searching

Les the writer, promoting his book A Card For The Clubs

Chapter Three

A Card For The Clubs

IN THE MEANTIME, DAWSON MANAGED TO CONTAIN HIS SURREAL HUMOUR LONG ENOUGH

to pass an audition and represent Manchester in a strange little talent competition to be held in the Hulme Hippodrome, a respectable theatre set in a vast sprawl of slums. Considering the old-fashioned nature of most cabaret turns, then as now, Dawson's act must have been truly astonishing.

He walked on-stage dressed as Quasimodo, complete with hump and scary leer. He crouched at a grand piano and proceeded to sing a song that was part off-key and comic, part childlike. He opened the piano lid and extracted a glass of coloured liquid, designed to look like some evil potion. Downing it, he fell into his gurning routine – which at least solicited a few embarrassed titters from the audience – and then crawled into the piano. He emerged from the other side of the piano wearing a ginger wig.

And that was it. Dawson took a bow and was met by the most deafening silence he had ever encountered. Thirty people were sitting before him, mouths open in disbelief and no idea of how they were supposed to react to such a bizarre spectacle. Indeed, having never experienced such off-beat humour, they simply couldn't comprehend what they were seeing. Worse, for Dawson, was the fact that he had invited his mum and dad to see the event and to marvel at their preposterously gifted son. On finishing his act, he looked for them but they had swiftly departed. When he arrived home, that evening, the front door opened and he was swiftly hauled inside. 'Get in here before any bugger sees you,' said his mother, 'You are a bloody embarrassment to us.'

Defeated and humiliated, his confidence slipping to a new low, Les Dawson rather unsensationally quit showbiz. Grasping reality with both hands, he became a door-to-

Letting it all hang out in anti-glam mode

When You're Smiling

The original inspiration for Ada? Great British comedian Norman Evans

A Card For The Clubs

door Hoover salesman. Unwittingly, he had stumbled into another unorthodox training ground. Selling Hoovers, he soon discovered, required a great deal of 'performance'. To his delight, he found that this gave him plenty of room to improvise and, generally speaking, people seemed to warm to his little act. They didn't buy his Hoovers, but they had a good time.

Actually, I do him a slight disservice here. There were days when Dawson staggered home, thoroughly sickened by the whole process and with no orders to present to his increasingly irritated boss the next day. Then he would lock into a decent run of sales. Enough to keep him in employment, but hardly enough to win the 'salesman of the year' award. He was moved, rather spitefully, to Moss Side, a dense web of streets stretching from the dank slums of Hulme to leafier Whalley Range and arguably the most deprived area of the city.

'The Moss' was, even then, fraught with dangers for the wandering stranger. In Moss Side, his job included more and more general maintenance, fixing washer pipes while glancing across the cellars, watching the rats scurry from hole to hole. He was thoroughly miserable during this period in his life. The only relief came from his night-time stints on the piano, though often the misery pursued him there as well, forcing him to drink himself into a numbing stupor. It was the warm glow at the end of a long day. Despite the drink, or perhaps because of it, Dawson punctuated his performances with snatches of poetic comedy. It didn't necessarily go down too well, especially in tap rooms more concerned with the darts or pub billiards than listening to some ivory tinkler – 'I reckon 'is piano needs tunin' anyway' – warbling in the corner and telling weird stories.

Hoover sales were hardly booming and he left the job, once again disillusioned. It seemed that little would ever go right for the young Les. One thing was for sure, he wasn't a natural salesman, although he knew he would miss visiting the people in their homes. He hardly ever failed to strike a chord with them. In fact, his chatty bonhomie was altogether too cheerful for the job in hand.

'I'd started feeling sorry for them and I'd realise that the last thing they needed was a new Hoover,' he confessed later. 'I always felt that I was too close to the people. It was the same as in the boxing. No killer instinct. It was a definite fault of mine.'

In the early 1950s, Dawson, still searching for 'something', responded to his recurring wanderlust and left for London. He found a flat over a café in Battersea, exactly the kind of place you end up with in London when you arrive for the first time, stony-broke.

When You're Smiling

Astonishingly, during this period he was to meet and befriend the great comic Max Wall. Wall, at this stage battling with a career well past its peak, still managed to take Dawson under his wing as a protégé of sorts, although Les Dawson never quite understood what was required of him. He would later refer to this as 'one of the oddest periods of my life.'

Those who believe in fate may sense that some kind of baton was passed on from the ailing genius to the burgeoning young talent, even though Les Dawson hadn't actually done anything in the way of comedy performance. We might speculate that there has to be a reason for this odd meeting. Well, there was. After singing for Wall, Dawson was sent to a voice trainer in Leeds who, after training him briefly, sent him straight back. This curious adventure preceded a major hiccup at the start of Les Dawson's showbiz career. He was a singer. He was back in London. Broke. And suddenly, from nowhere, came a telephone call. He was told to hotfoot it across London. Max Wall wanted to see him, fast. This, perhaps, was the moment when surrealism truly entered Les Dawson's life. Wall told him that, due to a musician's strike, the singer Edmund Hockridge had been told to pull out of Max Wall's television show. And Max wanted Les to stand in. In a dream, Les was shunted before photographers, before Fleet Street, before PR people. His name flickered in the *Evening Standard*, in the *Daily Mirror*. He was suddenly in. And then, just as suddenly, the strike ended before he had even rehearsed. Edmund Hockridge took up his position once more… and Dawson was cast aside. How cruel, to be within an inch of a BBC live television programme, so unexpectedly, and to have it whisked away.

How cruel indeed. In a Battersea pub that evening, Les Dawson watched the television show and steadily drank himself senseless. Within a week he was washing dishes in a Lyon's Corner House at night, scouring the theatrical agencies by day. He soon returned to Manchester, to familiarity, to poverty, but also to the cushion of family love.

The mythical glamour of writing did, at least, appear to be within reach when Dawson was accepted as a cub reporter for the *Bury Press* in North Manchester. Better, surely, than flogging vacuum cleaners? Dawson was ecstatic. Culturally, it was as far from the Left Bank as it is physically possible to get. Bury in the late 1950s was still the soot-blackened heart of Lancashire and still bore the scars of the industrial revolution. It was also still a place where spades were called spades and pretentious wordsmiths received short shrift.

A Card For The Clubs

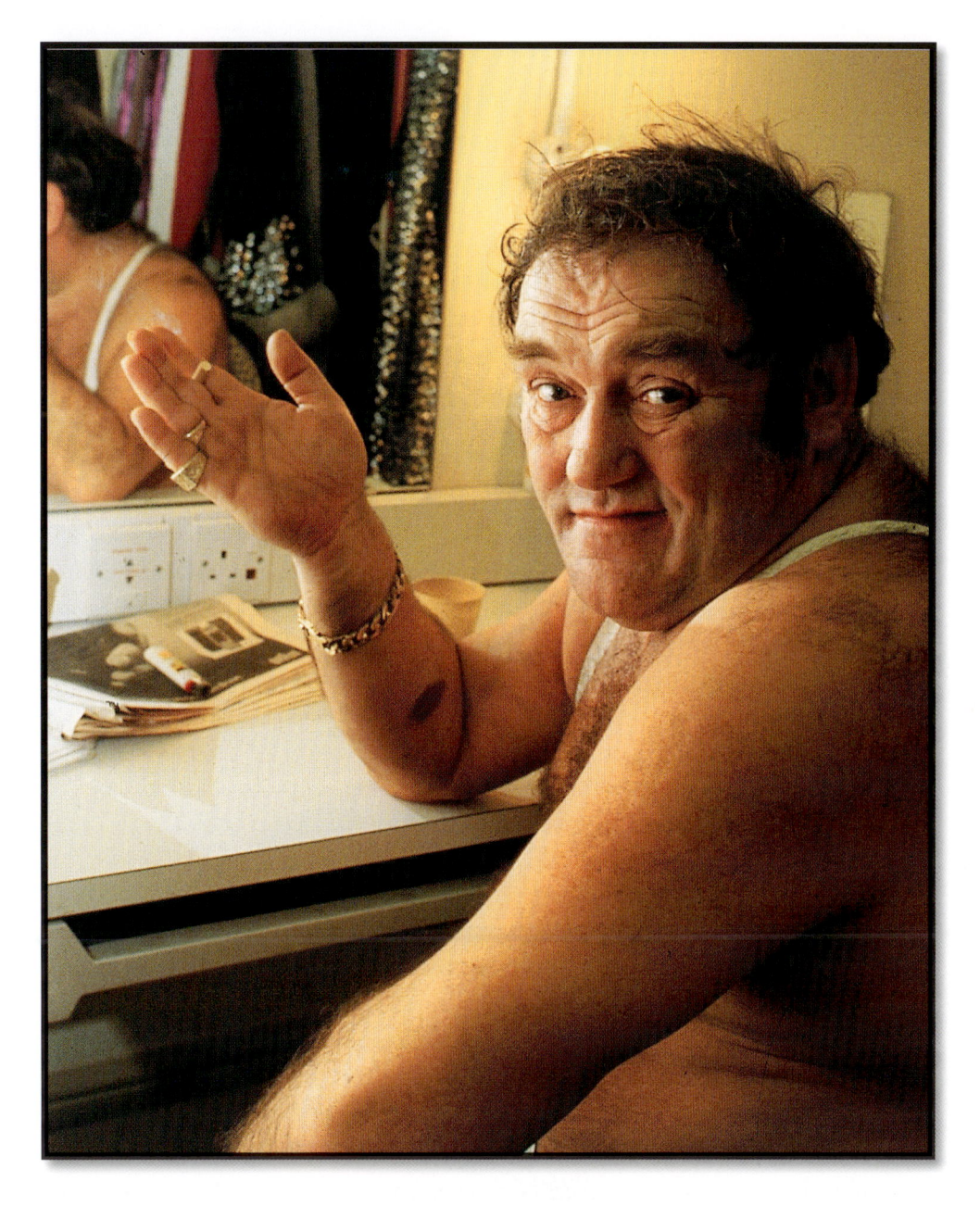

Dressing room angst

None of that clouded Dawson's brow, as he later recalled:

> 'I went to cover the funeral of an alderman. I had me pencil and me book. I was going to make my name in journalism. Anyway, I went to cover this guy's funeral and I cribbed a piece from Hindenburg's funeral. The thing was, in my head, I was this fantastic, descriptive writer. As it happened, I was pathetic. I wrote, "The clouds glowered down on the tear stained pavements of Kablesk." I was really proud of it. I took it into the office and I was so naïve I really thought they would be thrilled. I thought they would think that they had discovered a great poet. So I gave it to the sub-editor and he took one look at it and said: 'What a load of crap. Eeee lived and Eeee deed, that's all thee needs to know.' I lost interest after that.'

He meant it, too. If journalism was the art of presenting facts directly, and all too often it's precisely that, then Dawson was its antithesis. He loathed direct reportage especially because, as he soon realised, it was only concerned with the attention-grabbing angle rather than the less sexier truth. No. From the outset, Dawson was a words man. And from the outset, literally since primary school, he found this a lonely fascination indeed. Yet his experience on the *Bury Times* served to strengthen his resolve. The attitude angered him. He knew that he was not James Joyce, but he had an identifiable talent. He could use words to take people on an incredibly strange diversion but then, all of a sudden, switch back to grim reality. It was the essential Les Dawson comedy trick and nobody else, absolutely nobody, worked it as brilliantly as him. It was not just timing. It was the screwed-up face. It was the dour Mancunian growl. It was all the grief of trying to find a trace of romance on a wet Tuesday afternoon in Ancoats.

Not easy. It was the flip side of L.S. Lowry. It was hopelessness taken to an absurd extreme. At first, people, didn't know what to make of Les Dawson. Later, it would dawn on them. There is humour in everything, however unlikely, and Les could find it. There is humour in the biscuit counter of Ashton-Under-Lyne's indoor market, if you search hard enough. If you use that imagination. Before long, as the 1950s moved uneasily into the birth of the rock 'n' roll age, Les was taking his act through the clubland of the north of England.

*   *   *

A Card For The Clubs

The Northern Working Men's Clubs

Not easy places to play, in the 1990s, unless you slip into a 1960s parody, or glam up with wigs and flares for a 1970s spectacular, or even slap on some 1980s eyeliner. To perform well is still to play to the audience's expectations. There is nothing wrong in this, nor in the undemanding manner of the crowd. They want easy, identifiable entertainment. In the 1950s, early 1960s even, this hunger for the expected wasn't just something in the prevailing air, it was something that was demanded. For acts great or lowly, the brief was simple. Get on. Fit in. Get off before the bingo. Come back on. Don't mess with last orders. Many of these clubs, from Warrington to Doncaster, from Preston to Derby, were vast brick chasms, thick with cigarette smoke and run on a draconian schedule. The entertainment was ruled completely by the social habits of the clientele. And the clientele were the gods. They paid the wages. Artists bowed to their every reactionary whim. You can easily imagine nearly all the comedians who broke through on early 1970s television, the entire, low-brow mass of them, slotting perfectly into this militaristic schedule. It was their schooling.

But not Les Dawson. It is difficult to conceive of Les Dawson fitting into this particular scheme of things. It defies belief. They wanted quick-fire jokery. Instead, they got slabs of sheer surrealistic beauty – such as this:

> 'Last evening, I was sitting at the bottom of my garden, smoking a reflective cheroot, when I chanced to look up at the night sky. As I gazed, I marvelled at the myriad of stars glistening like pieces of quicksilver cast ceaselessly on black velvet. In awe I watched the waxen moon ride like an amber chariot across the zenith of the heavens, towards the ebony void of infinite space, wherein the tethered bulks of Jupiter and Mars hung forever festooned in their orbital majesty. And as I stared in wonderment, I thought to myself, "I must put a roof on this outside lavatory",

Say what? OK, so it worked beautifully when delivered to the sophisticated audience watching, say, the *Michael Parkinson Show* in 1978. Then Les Dawson touched the viewers' own pretensions and brought them solidly back down to earth. Bang. Fantastic. But that was in the late 1970s. Les Dawson had been throwing such material around for twenty years beforehand.

When You're Smiling

His material was not entirely without precedent. If Les Dawson had an influence, it was the great Norman Evans, Lancashire's Ambassador of Mirth. As the years passed by and Dawson slowly built his act, bits of Evans would occasionally appear in his material.

Evans had appeared some thirty years before Dawson and likewise spent his early working years in obscure, sedentary jobs (at Arrow Paper Mills in Castleton, Rochdale, for starters). Unlike Dawson, however, he entered showbiz through the traditional route of the amateur operatic society. With the help of local lass Gracie Fields, Evans gained a foothold on the southern circuit. His genius revolved around the creation of characters he plucked directly from the streets of Rochdale, such as the wonderful Joe Ramsbottom, from the celebrated sketch, 'The Dentist' – the perfect gentle caricature of the working-class man in the street with attitude. Unlike Les Dawson, Evans' performance was more of an acting role, though he too used words to creative effect. But the closest parallel came with another Evans creation, Fanny Fairbottom, a gurning female housewife addicted to gossip. Every night she would climb on an upturned bucket and chat to an unseen neighbour in the ongoing sketch, 'Over The Garden Wall'. Here, undoubtedly, are the roots of Cissie and Ada. The lengthy routines, which always opened with the wall waiting mid-stage, would move into a clever, fast-moving monologue, with Evans cheekily using the language he had picked up on the street. He also managed to affectionately and accurately pick out the absurdities in the comments of middle-aged housewives, the true rulers of working-class society.

Les Dawson fell uneasily into the working men's club circuit. A dream of future success rather than stardom fired his act, although the circuit seemed increasingly frustrating. At every club, he met the same cynical attitude. 'Who do you think you are? We've 'ad some of the greats working here. Our customers want to know what time the pies arrive.' And, just occasionally, 'You'll never work in showbiz again.' That happened, on nights when Dawson just couldn't connect and his material soared straight over the audience's heads. He learnt lessons playing to those crowds that he would never forget.

That was the nature of Dawson's futile, almost existential trek through the north of England in the late 1950s, attempting to fit his increasingly surreal act into the rigid format of the clubs. He was in search of open minds. He found none, and so he reached his famous career trough. It occurred in 1956, in the gloomy and unforgiving Hull Trawlermen's Club which, incredibly, offered him a brief residency. It was, he would often dourly state, the most unsuitable venue on the face of the planet. It wasn't apathy he

A good impression of being a congenial host

faced on those occasions. It wasn't audience irritation, either. It was sheer hatred, a loathing so extraordinary it went beyond the absurd. His work, he repeatedly told himself, was edging into something different. It was a scenario paralleled nearly thirty years later, when the deadpan absurdist Ted Chippington specialised in inciting exactly the same reaction. But Chippington did it on purpose. At Hull, it was utter mayhem. Jeers drowned him the instant he strolled onstage, after which he entered a kind of nether world visited by few other artists. 'Listen mate, 'ave you ever thought about being a bricklayer?'

The Hull experience actually emboldened Dawson. Especially as, towards the end of his residency, the audience hostility began to subside. If he strained his ears he could even hear the odd faint chuckle. It may not seem like such a victory, but to Dawson it was a key moment in his career.

When You're Smiling

Les serves pregnant first wife Meg and mother-in-law, at Unsworth bungalow

'Hull changed my life completely,' he would remember later, 'and the reason is simple. Somehow I handled it and escaped with my dignity, and a couple of other things, intact. I realised, there and then, that nowhere in the whole world would I find an audience as tough as that. If you can handle Hull, you can handle anything.'

It could easily have destroyed him. Indeed, it nearly did. But after Hull, even the most desultory audiences seemed comparatively pliable. He could work them.

The northern club circuit is considered a harsh environment for comics. In fact, its mythical 'hardness' is exaggerated, although every comic has a tale to tell similar to Les Dawson's. He, however, wasn't learning the ropes in the way comics usually develop in the club circuit. He was genuinely producing something that had never been seen before, and that people didn't know how to react to.

The Manchester club circuit, at least, had warmed towards him. He trod the boards wherever they would have him, and some of the places he appeared at were distinctly odd. For a start, he regularly played The Russell Club, in Hulme, which was re-invented twenty years later as The Factory Club, the epicentre of the late 1970s Manchester music scene. He performed on bills with such unknowns as Jimmy Tarbuck and… well, Jimmy Tarbuck, anyway. It wasn't a full-time occupation. Selling Hoovers once again occupied his days, although his sales pitch verged on the absurd. Hoover selling was, however, a dubious method of keeping a steady income. Dawson broke too many rules, rehearsing his act on his customers and upsetting the Hoover hierarchy.

Then, one night, he went to Crumpsall, a particularly dour district, bordering Collyhurst and Moston. The venue was The Crumpsall Labour Club and the evening was to be a private party. The portents were not good. However, the club turned out to be surprisingly welcoming, the food fairly decent, with free meat pies on offer. Les ate one, and looked up. The club's booker, Peter Osgood, sauntered across arm in arm with his girlfriend, a slim, attractive girl called Margaret Plant. She asked Les if he wanted to use a clavoline, a device which could make a piano sound like the horrible organs that were deemed strangely enticing in working men's clubs. Les replied, not untypically, 'I've already been.'

Not the greatest joke in the world, but a reasonably decent chat-up line. Although Margaret didn't think so. She spun around on her high heels and strode off. The evening turned out to be one of Les's worst. The microphone failed. The jokes fell limp and lifeless to the floor. Margaret Plant, in particular, was less than impressed.

Shortly after this, Les embarked on a 'lad's night out' – a whole gang from the club went to the Northern Sporting Club – after which, they all drunkenly fell into an Indian restaurant. In 1958 this was an exotic climax to a riotous evening. Here, much to his amazement, Les again encountered Margaret Plant. He invited her to the following day's Hoover staff dance and, after some indecision, she agreed to go. Les Dawson had met the first of the two true loves of his life. Margaret, at his insistence, soon became the less formal Meg. The couple swiftly fell deeply in love, and were married on 25 June, 1960. Something very right had happened in Les Dawson's life at last.

*   *   *

Chapter Four

Broadcasts And Broadsides

TO HER CREDIT, MEG SENSED THAT, DESPITE INDICATIONS TO THE CONTRARY, LES DAWSON WAS FOLLOWING HIS DESTINY.

It would have been easy for Meg to rein Les into a 'normal' job and domestic entrapment. Yet not once during the following nine years of hard, fruitless slog did Meg fail to encourage and support her husband's showbiz 'career'. Theirs was an extraordinary partnership. Not a hint or a flicker of showbiz glamour enriched those early years. Les abruptly, courageously, left Hoover, which wasn't easy. Ironically, he had become rather fond of the job. He kept a foot in the art of sales, which he correctly believed to be a rich training ground for a would-be entertainer, and started to sell plasticware, from loo brushes to tea strainers.

He also tried to push further into showbiz. He was delighted when he secured a week as comic and compère in a *Billy Cotton Band Show* at the prestigious Manchester Opera House. However, his expectations were dashed when the show attracted small audiences and indifferent applause.

In his autobiography he described the scene as 'a silence like a forgotten grave in a disused cemetery.' Manchester Opera House was never the most forgiving of theatres.

He worked harder than most. He wrote endless letters, and reams and reams of wild surrealism, much of it quite naïve. Most radio and television producers, impresarios and club owners affected a cynical eye when approached by this new talent. Two pages of Dawson's nonsense, however delightful, wasn't exactly playing the game. Indeed, it would most probably have been seen as precocious and lacking in reverence for

Les often adopted character roles for sketches in his TV series

When You're Smiling

Larger than life. With Diana Dors

Broadcasts And Broadsides

showbiz tradition. I doubt that Les Dawson ever really put much store in reverence. He wasn't the forelock-tugging type, and one wonders if the sycophancy of the television world held much appeal for him. It was, I sense, something to be endured.

Mike Craig, former BBC Light Entertainment Producer, remembers: 'Les wrote a letter to Jim Casey, who was Head of BBC Light Entertainment in Manchester. Jim rang me up and said, "Do you want to go and see a man called Les Dawson? He's working at a club in Oldham?" I said yes, although I had never heard of him.' Jim Casey, uniquely at the time, was touched by Dawson's extraordinary prose, which seemed so off-the-wall.

Mike Craig again: 'I had no idea what to expect, but Jim had obviously sensed something. He said: "This Les, he wrote me a letter and I was really impressed with it, in fact, anyone who can write stuff like this deserves seeing."

'He read the letter out. It was just incredible. Something like, "Dear Jim. I have just recently returned from a tour of the African rain forest, appearing with Martha Hagerty's Romany trombone dwarfs." I don't think that Jim had ever encountered anything remotely like that before.'

Perhaps luckily for Les, Jim Casey had a great love of the English language. He was also rather bored by the comics then on the club circuit. Indeed, the reactionary nature of the clubs made them, I believe (perhaps controversially) a poor training ground for entertainers who would eventually move into television. True, it would help build a solid professionalism. It would help them build a cast iron act, too, a solid lump of material that would pander to the needs of the crowd. It was an insurance thing and, although it would be encouraged by agents who wanted to see their acts working the circuit, causing no upset, and earning decent revenue, it would stifle genuine creativity and innovation.

Dawson was riding the downside of this. As the audiences didn't know his name or his act, and had no awareness of the type of act he was about to unleash upon them, it is not in the least bit surprising to discover that the response was lukewarm. At least then he could sneak quietly away, or go for a drink at the bar unbothered by well-wishers.

Jim Casey: 'The audiences didn't like Les at all in the early days. They just didn't want him. He used to come to my office, really down. He'd tell me that he was packing it all

Overleaf: Kitchen sink drama with Thora (Hird) and Ted (Heath)

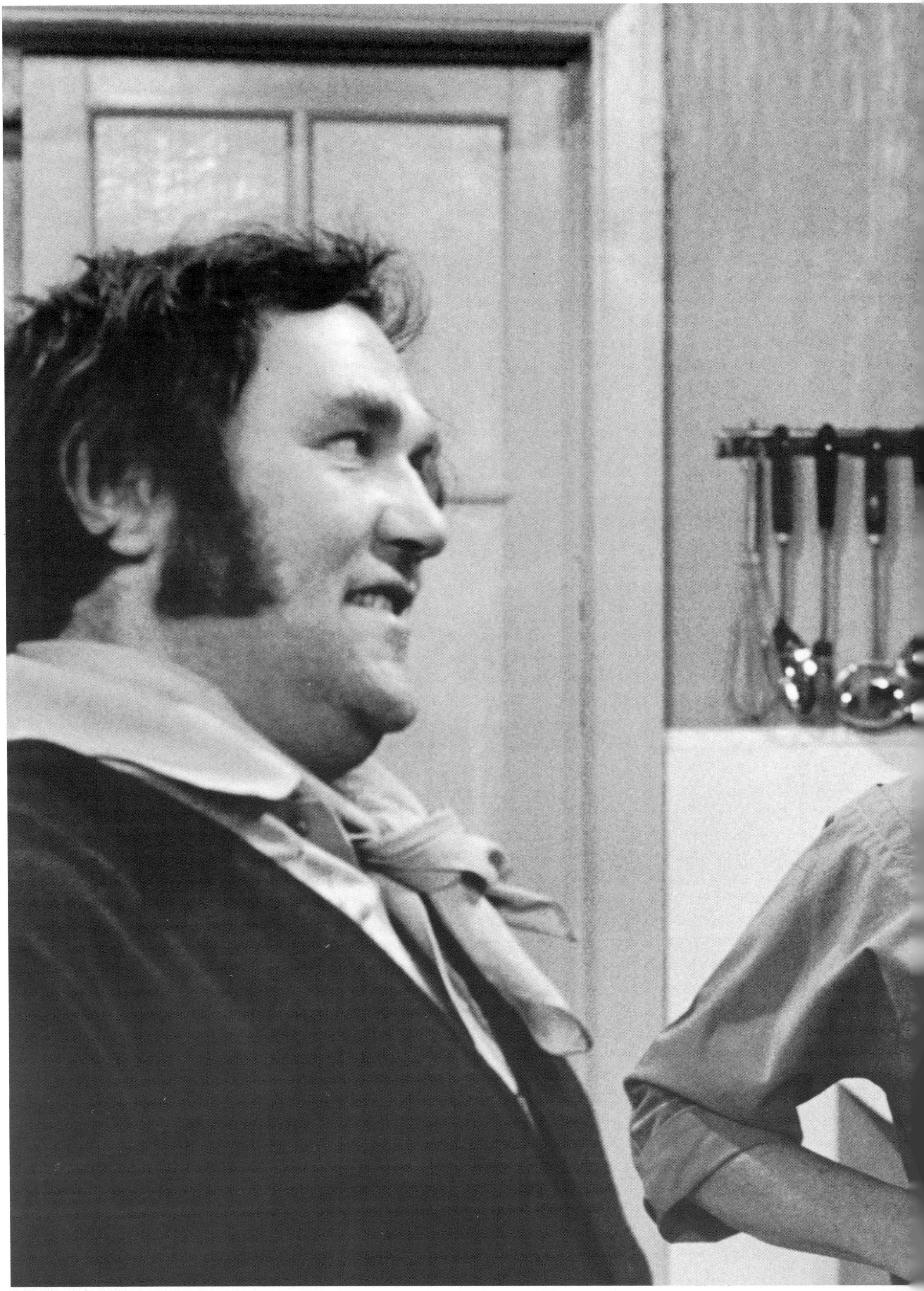

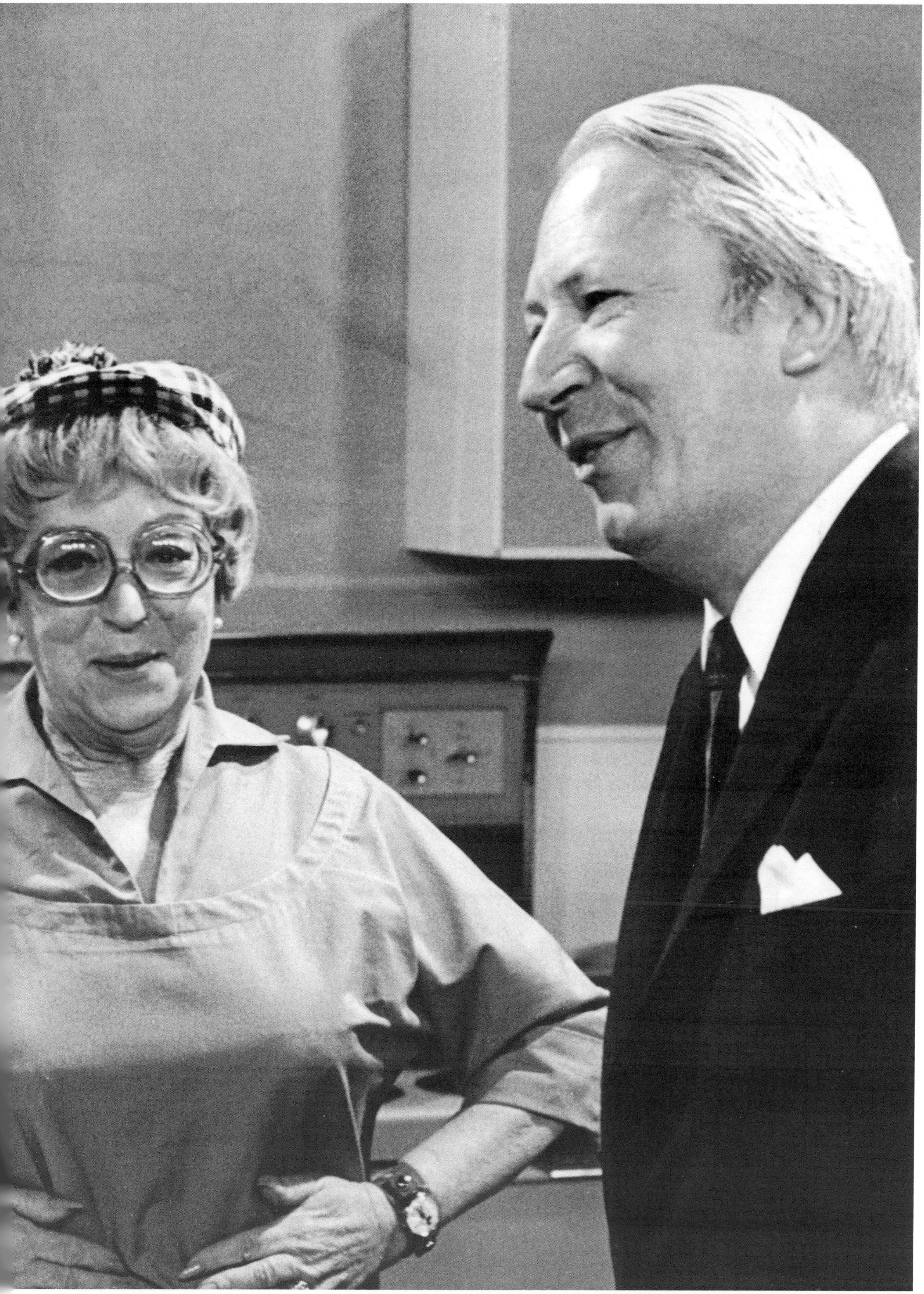

in, that he would have been better off selling vacuum cleaners. I used to try and gee him up. I'd tell him, "Les, you are going to be a massive star." But he'd say, "But they paid me off on Monday night." I'd tell him that those audiences weren't going to see him. They were going for other reasons and they just encountered him. He couldn't possibly expect them to understand but, one day, when they actually pay to see him and hear his long rambling stories, they would fall about. Which is exactly what happened. I always knew it would, because he was so obviously a unique talent. But, obviously, it was difficult to get him to see that. He just thought I was trying to lift his spirits.'

Roy Barraclough adds: 'Les wrote most of his own material. Certainly the stand up stuff. The off-the-wall stuff. I think, looking back, he was very much ahead of his time. I think in terms of 25 years ago, this sort of surreal material was very new indeed. Unheard-of, really. It must have taken great courage to stand up in front of audiences and deliver that stuff, because they didn't really want to hear it at all. They just wanted to hear jokes. They would sit in total silence. I don't think they knew what the hell he was on about.'

An example of the Dawson prose style in full effect:

> 'I boarded the grime-smeared and vandalised charabanc with some trepidation,' Les wrote in *Les Dawson's Lancashire*. 'It was so old the driver admitted that it didn't run on petrol; it went along on a mixture of swamp gas and bat droppings. I was also slightly apprehensive when I saw that the mudguards were thatched. In a series of coughs and barks, the primeval pantechnicon lurched away from the bus depot with all the grace of an arthritic gypsy fiddler with chilblains. The seats were so hard we had to take out insurance for poor circulation and buttock cramp.'

Jim Casey again: 'Les loved old English novels. He would get a phrase from these and he would work on it. I remember him one day saying to me, "Listen to this, Jim, isn't this wonderful?" And he read this phrase: "I will render you asunder with a ball from my horse pistol." He always used these kind of phrases and the fact that he put them into ordinary everyday situations about the wife or the mother-in-law, that's what made him so different. There was no one else on Earth who was doing anything like that.'

Broadcasts And Broadsides

One typical instance took place in the nicotine-lined entertainment room of a large Victorian pub in Gorton. There is some confusion whether this pub was The Pamona, a moody slab of a pub near Reddish Bridge, or the Gorton Brook. Either way, we are talking about dour, foreboding interiors enlivened by occasional strips of tinsel, with a tiny stage patrolled by a viciously sarcastic compère. The room would be skirted by bench seats and tables, scattered with half-drained pint pots and smouldering ashtrays. In fact, smoke would fog the room, putting a certain distance between artist and crowd. An organ would bellow tunes of the day while singers of a sub-Humperdinck standard would attempt to infuse some romance into the proceedings. Wives would smile, husbands would light fags and cast their eyes to the heavens as soppy love dirges drifted through the pall.

Later, it would turn into the kind of organ-driven rock 'n' roll that has rarely been heard outside of the north of England. Believe me: if you want, you can still sample this rare hybrid today. It is rock 'n' roll with every essence of rhythm and blues drained carefully away. It is asexual and depressing, designed to subdue any trace of dangerous energy in the crowd. Before this, as the crooners wailed ineffectively into the blue smog, Les Dawson sat in his dressing room, itself about as enchanting as a mortuary, smoking profusely and working on his act. This scene could have been anywhere in the north. It is important simply because it was evocative, in its own way, endlessly fascinating and something that would shape the caricature of northernness that would enrich so many of Dawson's future monologues. He would saunter on cue to the centre of the stage to a ripple of applause. There was something intriguing and pathetic about the whole spectacle, and Dawson, rather than fighting this, would actually attempt to enhance it. And it was here that his glorious self-deprecating style would take hold. Far better to follow that sarcastic ripple with his own brassed-off sneer. 'Thanks. I've seen the Grim Reaper get a better welcome than that.'

It was a way of working through the apathy, working with it and, quite possibly, getting off that stage with dignity intact. It also helped him to write. Had he received a warm welcome, he would probably have fallen into a routine stacked with cheery banter, thereby losing that edge that made him a true original in the world of stand-up comedy.

Without the foresight of Jim Casey, it is difficult to see how Dawson might have got out of that deadening circuit. Honing his act was one thing; selling it to clubland was quite another. Sooner or later, the careering about from one sullen club to another would surely have thinned to nothing. What's more, he knew it. He had to find a way of reaching beyond the limited scope of single live appearances. It was the 1960s. He had to get on to radio or television. The only problem was that every tenth-rate Mike Yarwood-inspired impersonator seemed to be ahead of him in the queue. Jim Casey was fully aware of this and, trusting Dawson's talent, started to offer him short spots on the BBC's Light Programme, the precursor to Radio One. It wasn't much, and it didn't exactly dispel Dawson's fear of failure, but it helped. It was a sign that things might improve. What's more, and to the amazement of his neighbours and friends, some of these radio shows were household names. Suddenly, Les Dawson wasn't just someone who 'entertained' in some little club, somewhere in the north. His short, sharp spots, truncated monologues and extended jokes, shone like diamonds among time-honoured radio institutions such as *Workers' Playtime* and *Midday Music Hall*.

These appearances were the making of Dawson on radio. It was an unfamiliar medium, but Casey knew that it was one where Dawson's wordplay would be most effective. It's so simple: people listen to the radio. In order to sell this act, this voice, Dawson's words would have to be heard first. It was a slow process. Short bursts of radio would hardly make him a star, but it was a move in the right direction. Cleverly deflecting Dawson's understandable worries – he was becoming heartily sick of working the clubs – Casey continued to filter the comic into the radio schedules. At times, the broadcasts only went to the north of England, but this didn't matter. It was all experience. Casey even wrote a short series, *Dawson – Man Of Fiction*, which tested Les's 'radio presence' to the full, using his voice to great dramatic effect. Only when he believed Dawson had the necessary radio confidence did Casey proceed with his plan. He contacted the Head of Light Entertainment, at Broadcasting House and suggested a pilot show, based around Dawson, for the Light Programme. It was to be a showcase, of sorts, recorded at the BBC's Playhouse Theatre in Hulme. Although in retrospect this still seems a modest break, it gave Dawson a massive personal boost. More importantly, his name started to reverberate around the tight circle of nationally famous comedians. He wasn't a star, yet, but people in the business began to sit up and take notice.

In his book, *Look Back In Laughter Volume Two*, Mike Craig recalled the time when Les Dawson appeared as a guest on a comedy panel game from this period, based at the ABC Studios in Birmingham. The show, *Strictly For Laughs*, was chaired by the godfather of BBC radio comedy, Kenneth Horne. This, too, was a sign that Dawson was moving in the right

Broadcasts And Broadsides

Two northern icons; Les and Cyril Smith

circles. But there were also signs that this new talent, not too far from middle age by now, wasn't the normal bundle of ambition and neuroses. As Mike Craig explains, 'On the first show, one of the panellists was Les. I remember him walking into the Green Room, as the other comics were bragging about their various forthcoming TV spots, series, tours abroad, summer seasons, royal shows, etcetera. Kenneth knew they were all trying to outdo one another and so, timing his interjection to perfection, he turned to Les with a marvellous twinkle in his eye said, "So, tell me Les, what are your plans for the future?"

'Les replied in his own inimitable way, "Well, Kenneth, in among the dross of the northern working men's club circuit, there is a shaft of white light. Jim Casey wants to do a pilot radio show with me in Hulme."'

When You're Smiling

It was to prove Dawson's pivotal moment. In his words to Kenneth Horne, Dawson had already turned the corner. The pilot show was, in his eyes, the doorway out of his nightly club work. As he would later tell Radio Four:

> 'I was desperate at that point. The radio work wasn't much, but it gave me something to cling to. I had decided that the club audiences were never going to accept me. Strictly speaking, some of them did, but I didn't want to be doing that for the rest of my life. I will be forever grateful for the BBC, and Jim, for giving me something to cling to. Without that, I would have gone slowly insane. They just speeded up the process a bit.'

It was Meg who encouraged Les to audition for *Opportunity Knocks*. The crucial moment came on a Sunday night, as Les mooched on the sofa, watching *Sunday Night At The London Palladium* on TV, noticeably wincing every time Jimmy Tarbuck, who had climbed steadily above Dawson since their shared engagements around Manchester, managed to send the audience into hysterics. It was a painful sight and Meg was duly moved. 'You want to be on there, don't you?' she scolded him, adding, 'Then do something about it. Write and audition for *Opportunity Knocks*.'

Although meant kindly (in fact, it would be the one action that catapulted Dawson into our homes) it was still demeaning for a professional comedian to audition for a talent contest, televised or otherwise. *Opportunity Knocks* had thrust a great many stars into the public eye, although more often than not they would proceed to sink without trace. Most of the acts were amateurs and, frankly, amateurish. That, one always cynically sensed, was the true appeal of the show. But Dawson knew that *Opportunity Knocks* might help put him on a level pegging with Tarbuck. Unknown to Dawson, he had already met the producer, Royston Mayoh, during brief television stint with Mike and Bernie Winters. For Dawson, that was a forgettable experience. Mayoh, on the other hand, was privately rather struck by this unusual northern comic and, seeing his name scribbled beneath another lengthy letter, persuaded presenter Hughie Green to give Les a go.

He passed. In March of 1965, ABC Television summoned him to the Didsbury Studios where *Opportunity Knocks* was filmed. It was to be the show's most celebrated moment. Although not strictly accurate, it was regarded as the first sighting of Les Dawson on

Broadcasts And Broadsides

British Television – certainly, it was the first time that Dawson ever connected with a television audience. Years later it would still be dragged out for Christmas Specials or comedy theme evenings. Any excuse, really, to see it once more. This is how it went.

Dawson was seated at a piano. 'Tonight I would like to play something from Chopin, but I won't. He never plays any of mine. Then I toyed with the idea of playing Ravel's 'Pavane Pour Un Infante Défunte', but I can't remember if it is a tune or a Latin description for piles. Anyway, before anyone slides into a coma, I'll play a song that was written by Bach as he lay dying. [Plays one note.] Then he died.

'The neighbours love it when I play the piano. They often break my windows to hear me better… My father was musical, he collected old instruments. The police often asked him if he had still got the loot [lute]… Dad spent so much time in prison, when they did finally release him, the governor asked him to go back, part-time… Mother used to sit me on her knee and I'd whisper, "Mummy, mummy, sing me a lullaby do." She'd say, "Certainly, my wee bundle of happiness. Hold my beer while I fetch me banjo."'

It is impossible to imagine this being performed without Dawson's unique, curmudgeonly delivery. Who else could get away with that loot/lute joke? But the Didsbury crowd erupted that night and Dawson left the stage as the 'clapometer' soared off the register. (Did anyone ever check if there was anything remotely accurate about that bizarre instrument, even though, as Hughie would often inform us, 'It is only for fun, it's your votes at home that really count'?) In Les Dawson's case, these words were particularly poignant, as he easily won in the studio, for fun, but lost in the postal vote. Not that it mattered a jot. Les Dawson had arrived. It was the start of a happy period for Dawson, as at last his professional life began to take form. The same year also saw the birth of Meg and Les's daughter, Julie. At last the dark days of self doubt were starting to fade.

*   *   *

Chapter Five

Knickers, Knackers, Knockers

LES ACCEPTED THE CHANCE TO WORK A SUMMER SEASON IN DOUGLAS ON THE ISLE OF MAN, APPEARING AT THE FOOT OF A BILL INCLUDING VAL DOONICAN AND JACKIE TRENT.

For the north-west of England in the mid-1960s, the Isle Of Man, full of fairy glens and quaintness, was still regarded as the most exotic of holiday destinations. Affordable and comparatively warm – it lies in the Gulf Stream – and bristling with curious Manx culture, it had the feeling of being foreign without all the problems of having to mix with real foreigners. And Douglas was like a tiny, cleaner Blackpool. Dawson was in his element. By day pushing his daughter's pram up and down the lovely promenade and at night settling into an act that played to packed houses. Contentment simply dripped from him, at times threatening to transform the curmudgeon who stalked the stage.

Back in the north, the 'family' moved into 2 Bradley Drive in the Unsworth district of Bury. A bungalow, complete with a small garden and a spartan collection of furniture. It wasn't much, as his income was still unsteady, but it was a start.

The radio shows trickled on until, in a move that would shift Dawson's career into a higher gear, he tried out for a show that would eventually reach the television screens as *Blackpool Night Out*. The try-out, although successful, was marred by misfortune – a lighting rig fell on a crew member. He wasn't seriously hurt, but the portents weren't good. For the first actual transmission, the show's star, Dickie Henderson, had to struggle

Cosmo Smallpiece, looking unusually composed

When You're Smiling

Ladies Man. With the Three Degrees

to capture the audience's attention, something nobody was expecting. Fired by his nerves, Les Dawson strolled to centre-stage and completely stole the show. Even Cliff Richard and The Shadows, at the very peak of their success, couldn't compete. It was a remarkable coup, but the truth was that Dawson had connected with the true heart of his audience, his eventual fan base. He had connected with Blackpool. The crowd's reaction was quite extraordinary. At last he felt like a success, and he would be forever grateful to Blackpool for that feeling.

After this, everything changed. As if by magic, his phone started ringing and wouldn't stop. Opportunities fell over themselves. His gleeful agent became accustomed to saying 'no' rather than snatching any chance that might flutter by. Other things happened, too, strange things indeed. People would nudge each other as he wandered through the shops of Bury. Wherever he went, recognition would cross passing faces, sometimes with

Knickers, Knackers, Knockers

irritating consequences. Fame had finally crept into his everyday life. It had its downside – it was scary and unsettling – but it was also exhilarating. Suddenly, the future was a kaleidoscope of limitless possibilities. To steady himself, Les upped his drinking. A second date at Blackpool swiftly followed. Same reaction. Same high. And then, wrenched from his family, Les Dawson surged through the British television schedules with dizzying speed, appearing with Cilla Black, Val Doonican and Billy Cotton.

He topped the bill, for the first time, in his first pantomime in Doncaster. Compared to the great panto successes that would become the Dawson trademark in the next twenty years, it was a modest and low-key affair, co-starring The Rockin' Berries, one of the many Merseybeat outfits who had slipped into the limbo of end-of-the-pier cabaret. Nevertheless, the show bounced happily from Doncaster to Stoke to Gloucester, providing Dawson with his first real experience of the rolling nature of an ongoing show. It had ad lib opportunities by the score and countless opportunities to experiment in front of crazed, screaming hordes of chocolate munchers. And their kids were even worse.

The summer of love, 1967, never actually reached Blackpool. Instead, the holidaymakers flocked to see variety shows. Rarely in the vast scope of light entertainment has the word 'variety' seemed more apt than the show which featured that year on the Central Pier. Both geographically and spiritually, Central Pier is the heart and soul of Blackpool. Les Dawson, now proudly middle-ranked in a bizarre bill which included the esteemed though rather dull American singer, Solomon King – 'She Wears My Ring' was his hit, if you were starting to scratch your head – the British street busker and, latterly, pop star, Don Partridge – 'Rosie, Oh Rosie', and others – plus sharp-tongued comic Ray Martine. None of them, it might be said, could be deemed at all suitable for a damp and demanding Blackpool used to Cilla and Des. It was a bizarre, ill-fitting mix of acts but, for Dawson, who couldn't put a foot wrong in Blackpool, the resultant chaos only served to highlight his professionalism and, indeed, his effortless link with the Blackpool people.

Life was fast, too fast at times. The birth of a son, Stuart, flashed by while, in between shows, in pubs and cafes, Les gathered his clubland memories together and segued them into a novel: *A Card For The Clubs*.

A further turning point was to come when Dawson, appearing on a Christmas bill in Leeds which also featured The Bachelors and Norman Collier, came off-stage and bumped into a tall young man wielding a cricket bat. The man was John Duncan.

When You're Smiling

Jim Casey's role as a massive and profound influence over Les Dawson's career would soon be passed on to Duncan, an energetic producer at Yorkshire Television. Duncan was very much in the same vein as Casey. He believed in encouraging original talent. That may not seem, at first, so unusual, but for an early 1970s television producer it was positively unique. The light entertainment/populist side of the television schedules was notoriously conservative in its approach. This isn't surprising, as the BBC/ITV ratings war, which now seems almost quaintly simplistic, was so precariously balanced that one false move, one slab of entertainment that didn't slot neatly into the expectations of viewers weaned on Val, Cilla and Rolf, would produce that stiff and ominous click as the TV switch changed channels. Innovation was generally reserved for later in the evening. You didn't mess with peak time. John Duncan didn't exactly plan to revolutionize this area, but he did have a passion for television programmes that encouraged and made stars out of original talents. He had noticed Les, as most television people had, on Barry Cryer's lovely old radio show, *Jokers Wild*. Again, this is recalled in Mike Craig's *Look Back With Laughter,* when Michael Aspel refers to *Jokers Wild* as a time when 'We'd all travel up to Leeds and listen to Les Dawson.'

John Duncan had designs on Les. He wanted to make a transformation. Duncan knew that the distance between this dour Lancastrian club entertainer and the sparkling if bland razzmatazz of a Cilla, Val or Des television spectacular was vast. But that was the central core of his plan: to pitch these two showbiz extremes together. Les Dawson, wandering across the stage, multi-coloured lights spinning to the left and right, the words 'SEZ LES' sparkling away in the background while glamorous girls danced around him. It was quite an absurd idea… and it worked to spectacular effect. It was 1967 and this was practically the first time that British audiences had seen such a show surrounding an act where the only cheese was in his sandwiches. It was 1970s television stretched to parodic effect. It was a dry kickback and, far from swamping Dawson, provided a hilariously glitzy format for him to present and develop his bone-dry delivery.

It would also mark, by happy accident, the debut of the celebrated Les Dawson/Roy Barraclough team, together in the kind of drag that would shame a panto in Mablethorpe. That enchanting twosome, Cissie and Ada, complete with leopard-effect headscarves and drooping bosoms.

Roy Barraclough explains: 'Cissie and Ada started in about 1974. We were working for Yorkshire Television on the very first *Sez Les* series. During the breaks in the studio,

Knickers, Knackers, Knockers

Sez Les with Sgt Cleese, who featured regularly in the series

waiting for the lighting, Les and I used to go into this routine because he was a big fan of Norman Evans, as was I. So we used to go into this routine and Les would say, "You'd get more life out of a 50-watt Mazda." And so on and so forth. But the producer, a lovely man called Bill Hitchcock, said, "That's a brilliant idea. Why don't you do that as a sketch and do the thing in drag?" We thought, no way. The public, surely, wouldn't be ready to see us two in frocks? But he asked us to try it as a warm-up. And that's what we did. We did a couple of weeks warming up the studio audience and it went down so well we decided to use it in the show.'

Roy Barraclough again: 'Les always tried to make me laugh and he would go to great lengths to try to make me laugh on camera. He was quite mischievous. I did a theatre season with him at Blackpool and we did a Cissie and Ada routine in the show which was

When You're Smiling

in a tea shop. He would have to pour the tea and he used to get a hip flask from up his leg and say, "Have a drop of this in your tea. You'll love it." All that kind of stuff. But every single performance he would find some terrible noxious potion, ranging from 100 per cent vodka to herbal remedies and all sorts of foul things which he would make me drink and he would twinkle and hope I'd start spluttering. But I would very bravely get on with the routine and ignore it all, keep a dead straight face. It was a real battle, sometimes. One day I had terrible flu and Les was always very fond of whisky. In the first half he would fill the cup with straight whisky… for my flu. Then, in the second half he poured in this thick red liquid. It was Benylin. I was comatose. They had to carry me out of the theatre and pour me into a taxi.'

Cissie and Ada were beautifully rounded, in every conceivable way. They could have come from any terraced street in Britain. Roy's social climber Cissie was the woman from the street's one detached house. The woman who had seen the bright lights, eaten pizza, coleslaw, spag bol. Cissie was a catalogue of the affectations that many working-class people sported, as post-war austerity wore off. And she grasped each new affectation with aplomb, using it as a stick with which to beat poor Ada, who was still blissfully stuck with a mid-century lack of pretension. Cissie was loosely based around an Annie Walker (of *Coronation Street*) character. She perused the broadsheets, peeled the labels off her brown sauce bottles, owned a gravy boat and almost certainly enjoyed prawn cocktails as her (evening) dinner-time starter. Ada, bless her, munched fish and chips from crumpled newspaper, saw adventure in a week at Skegness Butlin's and distrusted affectation in any form. Yet they were best mates, lost in banter.

They represented, one might say, the two halves of the twentieth century, although that might sound ludicrously grand. Ada was perfect Dawson. She was his kind of woman. If he met an Ada in Blackpool, as he often did, they would end up with their arms around each other's shoulders, drinking cups of tea and enjoying a riotous singalong. It would be gossip in the tea shop, stout in the snug bar. Les Dawson adored the Adas of this world.

Conversely, Roy Barraclough, a wonderful character actor, was more sophisticated than many of the characters he played. That's no put-down, quite the reverse, but Barraclough found a definite kinship with Cissie. The two were well balanced: they were as bright and as dim as each other:

Knickers, Knackers, Knockers

Cissie and Ada. 'Aving a right owd chinwag

When You're Smiling

Glamourpuss Ada

Knickers, Knackers, Knockers

Cissie: 'You're so pig-ignorant. Anyway, Leonard and I are going to the opening of *La Traviata* tonight.'
Ada: 'You won't catch me eating that foreign muck.'

Or, following Ada's surprisingly exotic holiday in Turkey:

Ada: 'Oh, Cissie, you've no idea what that food did to Bert and me.'
Cissie: 'Did you have the shish kebabs?'
Ada: 'From the moment we arrived.'

Now that is as gloriously, shamelessly daft as the hugely celebrated 'Oh infamy, infamy, they've all got it in fer me,' delivered by Kenneth Williams in *Carry On Cleo*.

Cissie and Ada created a whole new line of work, for Les Dawson if not Roy Barraclough, in comedy female roles. The whole of the second part of his career would be overshadowed by the pantomime dame. His accidental, Norman Evans-style, creation. One of the great comic inventions of the century. Some things are just meant to be.

Les was to discover that the course of television stardom, a seemingly trouble-free ride in the eyes of the viewers, in reality contained great highs and lows. One inevitably followed the other. The higher you climbed, the more inevitable the fall that awaited you. It was not an ideal scenario for those susceptible to bouts of anguish (i.e. every single television performer). The constant fear, for any comic, is of overexposure. This was especially true during the 1960s and 1970s when, with just three channels serving the nation, an act's potential penetration level was quite extraordinary; indeed, it would never reach such dizzy heights again. A star could be created in an instant. Equally, a solid reputation could be crushed by one ill-advised move. Television audiences wielded a mighty sledgehammer. And overexposure pushed the whole thing one step beyond acceptance and into the realms of viewer boredom. With television companies battling for ratings, the slightest slide could trigger a giant tumble, and nobody was sacred.

Les Dawson knew this in no uncertain terms. His act worked superbly in 1967, within the garish spectacle of *Sez Les*, but it was not to last. All too soon he seemed stretched, fighting to produce more and more material for that ravenous televisual audience. By the time the show reached its fourth series, the ratings started to dip and, to Dawson's dismay, so too did the size of his live audiences.

When You're Smiling

A couple of swells. Les with Shirley Bassey

A favourite Les Dawson anecdote apparently stems from this period. It is a true story and one which he would relate to friends, passing acquaintances – probably even my friend in the pub – and to anyone within earshot. It's a gem because, give or take the odd surreal embellishment, it could easily be the product of Dawson's imagination. It is dour, downbeat, and even slightly pathetic. Pure Les.

It concerns the letter he famously received one day, from the vicar of a small Yorkshire village. The letter was lengthy and as beautifully written as a particularly fine sermon. It told of how grateful the vicar and his wife felt for all the entertainment, the sheer pleasure, Dawson had given them over the years. Apparently, the couple had actually seen Dawson at a county show in nearby Bridlington and, oh, how thrilled they would be if he would consider being the guest of honour at the vicar's village fête. Les was truly moved. He called the thrilled vicar, made the arrangements and looked forward to a nice day out.

Knickers, Knackers, Knockers

When the day came, the weather was horrendous. Driving from Lytham across the Yorkshire Dales can be a real joy, but that's when the sun casts beams across the hazy valleys. It's not so enjoyable when the rain beats on your windscreen incessantly, as Yorkshire rain tends to do. To complete his misery, Les became hopelessly and infuriatingly lost. He tried to marry the vicar's directions with his Ordinance Survey map, but the two seemed to have little in common. When he finally arrived, the church was utterly deserted and there was a distinct lack of stalls and fête-like events on the surrounding common. Just before he was about to give up and leave, he dodged into the local newsagents who explained that due to the bad weather the entire thing had been switched to the local village hall. He finally arrived at the hall to find the entire village shivering, standing by radiators, clouds of steam rising from their drenched frames. The first remark he encountered was, 'It didn't rain when Vera Lynn came.'

Nonplussed, he clambered onto the makeshift stage. He made a nice little speech, full, he thought, of touching little observations of his journey across the Dales. And he felt good. He felt as if he had made a difference to the day, saved the fête from complete disaster. 'Thank you so much for coming,' the vicar concluded, 'thank you so very much because, believe me, we tried everybody.'

Although an extremely amusing anecdote, this hardly helped lift his spirits. Television success had stretched him to breaking point. To offset the anxiety, he admitted drinking a little too much, to Meg's growing annoyance.

It was Meg who was to persuaded him to make a brief appearance at a children's home in Buxton one day. Reluctantly, he arrived at the home feeling empty, and incapable of communicating the very warmth that had made him so successful in the first place. Two hours later, he left smiling. It was a simple and rather corny incident, but the kids in that home had instantly warmed to Dawson and succeeded in helping him out of his anxiety. So what if his ratings were falling? What kind of problems could he possibly have to compare with those smiling kids? He would often relate that story and, for once, neglect to embellish it with witty surrealisms. Once again, he had reached a turning point and, significantly, his work began to improve.

As did *Sez Les*. Series five included Cleo Laine, Shirley Bassey, David Essex and Olivia Newton-John. The top acts of the early 1970s, all happy to take a back seat to Dawson. Conscious of his luck, he worked tirelessly, honing his scripts. He wasn't stupid. He knew the show embraced daftness, he knew it teetered on the pale side of light, that it merely skimmed the surface of the darker comedy that flavoured his live act. But 1970s television was simply like that. Besides, *A Card For The Clubs* was picking up a scattering of decent reviews. It was a neat balance. The more thoughtful Les Dawson was reflected in those pages, while the television star continued to pursue a more shallow, but more tangible, fame.

Two more characters stole into Dawson's life. Another daughter, Pamela, was born to Meg and Les while, into the unreal world of *Sez Les*, he introduced a funny little persona, the beautifully-named Cosmo Smallpiece. He wouldn't have escaped with his sexual apparatus intact had he invented Smallpiece a few years later, when political correctness began rewriting history and comedy. But in the mid-1970s, the character was a creation of sheer delight. Taking a lead from the Benny Hill method of twisting the unrealistically high sex-drive of a squat, middle-aged man into a figure of fun, Dawson equipped Smallpiece with leery, thick glasses and a face that fell into a slobbering ogle at the merest whiff of a woman. When a woman came into sight, he would snap into his leery mode and announce the words, 'KNICKERS. KNACKERS. KNOCKERS'. But Cosmo was never a deviant. Never, in all his life, would he dare to actually touch a woman. But he was the ultimate voyeur. He was crushed by sex, wholly crushed, and appalling. He was the tiny little man who exists inside, one hesitates to suggest, almost every male on the planet. He was also, whatever the PC marines suggest, a fabulous comic foil for any glamorous woman who strode onto the *Sez Les* stage. But most importantly, Cosmo was very funny and a universal comic figure.

Luckily for Dawson, and indeed, for Cosmo Smallpiece, objections to this most basic character were minor. Indeed, Dawson seemed to transcend such arguments. As noted earlier, everyone always seemed to sense the warmth in him. He tells a wonderful story about a time, when at dinner in a plush West End restaurant, an extremely 'posh' lady complete with lackey in tow, sauntered haughtily up to him and announced, 'Mr Dawson, I have just one thing to say to you.'

Les looked at her, fearing the worst. 'Knickers. Knackers. Knockers,' she screamed, bursting into laughter. And it was Dawson who boldly stated, 'But that character is a sexual deviant.'

'Yes' she replied, 'But you know where you stand with him.'

This seemed to sum up the general view of the character, though there were a few exceptions. Yorkshire Television did receive a trickle, just a trickle, of venomous letters, supporting the feminist line and outlining what they would do to Les Dawson if they ever encountered him. However, Dawson's take on the battle of the sexes makes it very clear that he had only respect for women:

> 'Women generally are much more in control of things than men are. Really, the hand that rocks the cradle rules the world. Despite the feminists saying that men have always controlled everything, women have always been incredibly powerful. Most men hide behind an air of bravado.
>
> 'Surely no one could take my remarks that seriously? When I say my mother-in-law is a decoy for whaling ships, that her skin is stretched so tightly that when she bends her knees her eyelids fly open, I mean, come on! That is so existentialist it's ridiculous. To even believe I am being derogatory is crazy. It's cartoon imagery. It's a lampoon. It's basically affection, anyway. I don't pull anything to pieces that I don't like. Things I don't like I ignore. Things I'm fond of, I make fun of.'

Professor Jeffrey Richards suggests that 'When Les Dawson did mother-in-law jokes he was sending up the convention. When he talked about the mother-in-law, I think he did it with a twinkle in his eye and was sending up mother-in-law jokes. He was saying, "these are old-fashioned jokes and I am sending them up". He had that extra subtlety.'

It seems the idea of women as the pants-wearers permeated the Dawson household. Jim Casey: 'When Les was at home, writing one day, a fellow I knew was round at his house. Meg came in and said, "When are you going to mend that tap in the bathroom?" Les shrugged her off and she continued, "Don't just sit there. Go and fix it now."

'So he trundled off and fixed the tap and came back and started writing again. Then she would come in later and say, "It's 4.15. Go and pick the kids up." And he'd say, "Oh. all right Meg," and he went to get the kids. My friend couldn't believe his eyes.'

Meg's influence on Les was more supportive than restrictive. That said, her strong personality, unswayed by the sycophancy that was beginning to surround them both, and who was blind to the affectations that often consume showbiz families, won her many admirers within the business. Whenever Les and Meg attended functions together, which was often, they could be relied upon to battle through the platitudes and shallow chatter.

When You're Smiling

Roy Barraclough: 'He [Les] did a Royal Command Show at Windsor Castle and Meg was allowed to go as a guest. And at the party after the show, Les looked around and, to his utter horror, he saw Meg talking to the Queen and nodding away and pointing in various directions. He couldn't work out what she was saying. So, afterwards, he went to Meg and said, "I saw you talking to the Queen. What were you saying?"

She said, "I just asked her what kind of central heating she had. The Queen replied that she didn't know, so I told her she wanted to go on gas and, all those gaps under the doors, she should get them filled in because she was losing a lot of heat through them."

Les Dawson's first Royal Variety Performance came in 1973 when, almost to his embarrassment, he took his place on a bill which included Cliff Richard, Rudolf Nureyev, Dick Emery, Ronnie Corbett and, particularly poignant for a former jazz pianist, Duke Ellington. It was a dizzying roster of talents, preparing their acts with solid, professional dexterity. He wasn't to know, at that point, that, like him, nerves were twisting their insides into knots. That years of performance had taught them how to mask such tension. But it's there, bubbling ferociously behind the calmest of showbiz faces. For Dawson, new to this Royal Command lark, he knew he simply had to concentrate and allow his material to do the work for him.

To his chagrin, he realised that he was expected to walk on-stage seconds after it had been vacated by Rudolf Nureyev. It was, he kept telling himself, simply absurd. How could he hope… and then, before he realised what was happened, he was striding towards the microphone and launching into his most famous opening. Classic, classic Les Dawson: 'In 1645, Prince Rupert's mercenaries smashed Cromwell's left flank at Naseby and, in 1871, the Franco-Prussian war took a serious turn at the siege of Rouen and, in 1952, from the Kyles Of Bute, came the first report of an outbreak of sporran rash. None of this has anything to do with the act tonight, but it just shows how your mind wanders when you are worried.' It was the stuff of legend. Throwing the audience one way, and dragging them back with that simple last line. It even managed to cover for any visible signs of nervousness. It was quite the perfect opener for a first Royal Command Performance, at once easing him into his routine, establishing his rhythm.

After four minutes of verbally chastising his mother-in-law, injecting all the sharp little lines about mice throwing themselves on the traps, he proudly strode back to his dressing room, tension visibly rising from his shoulders. Les Dawson had truly arrived.

*   *   *

Knickers, Knackers, Knockers

Home for Christmas

Chapter Six

Under Attack

SEZ LES *HAD SERVED ITS TIME. IT WAS NOW* **1974** *AND, STILL* **CONTRACTED** *TO* **YORKSHIRE,**

Dawson and Barraclough embarked on a bold new tack. The idea, a 'one-off' or, if things went well, a pilot, was a brash situation comedy revolving around the package holiday industry and written by Ray Galton and Alan Simpson. Called *Holiday With Strings*, it also starred Molly Sugden and Patricia Hayes. The idea was simple enough: basically it was a *Sez Les* sketch stretched to half an hour and anchored by the magnetic interplay between Dawson and Barraclough. In *A Clown Too Many*, Les Dawson bemoans the fact that the writers are never allowed to extend the show into a short series, thereby exploring all the comedic possibilities. That said, *Holiday With Strings* would latterly be seen as a precursor to *Dawson's Weekly*, the six-parter written by the same team and, again, featuring Barraclough.

This was the show that estranged Les Dawson from some tabloid critics. It dawned on him that the relationship between his better work and his better critical notices was decidedly imbalanced. Furthermore, the press didn't share the public's new-found enthusiasm for his work, and maybe that was the point which hit the hardest. It may seem obvious nowadays that the media have to find the most dramatic angle and if this means slamming an artist as he reaches a peak of popularity, then that is what will happen. Conversely, some of Dawson's lesser work could receive glowing reviews and peripheral features. As *Dawson's Weekly*, a sharply written sitcom which took the *Holiday With Strings* formula a stage further, was mercilessly hammered in the press, Dawson's

The bronzed Adonis

75

When You're Smiling

The Dawson brood: With Meg, son Stuart and daughters Pamela and Julie

confusion turned to irritation. Throughout the rest of his life he would refer to his period with Yorkshire Television and, in particular, *Dawson's Weekly*, as his finest work. Rarely, however, has either sitcom resurfaced as a repeat. Rarely, too, have they survived in the misty nostalgic memories of the general public. From this point onwards, his relationship with the press in general would remains unsteady to say the least.

Famously, Les Dawson maintained an unfashionable respect for royalty, at one point rallying hotly against overtly 'politically correct' Manchester City Council's noticeable coolness towards the organisation of Princess Margaret's visit to Manchester's Palace Theatre in the mid-1980s. His royal links had been cemented ten years earlier, when his act caught the admiration of Prince Philip who would, unlikely as it may seem, remain a devoted Dawson fan, taking every opportunity to see the comic and seeing him out after the shows. Their relationship was founded in banter between comic and Prince, in which the north/south was lightly parodied. This had been forged during a televised show at Caesar's Palace in Luton, where Dawson had featured alongside pathos singers Peters And Lee and archetypal seventies dancer Peter Gordino, complete with his gyrating girls. After the show – a success, despite the dubious cast – the stars lined up, nervously awaiting the arrival of the Prince. Enthusiastically greeting Dawson, Prince Philip launched into light banter about the north of England and, in particular, Rochdale. At that Pennine town, the Queen had been presented with a bag of black puddings. 'They were delicious,' remarked Philip, 'We had them fried for breakfast.'

Unable to contain himself, Dawson replied to the effect that they should always be boiled. 'Nonsense, Dawson,' replied the Prince, 'you fry the blessed things.'

Now, perhaps as an icebreaker, this little argument would return every time Les Dawson met Prince Philip from that point onwards. (Les Dawson would later remark, 'I had to stand up for northern principles and they shouldn't mess with our black puddings.' This, itself, might be seen as a curious remark, perhaps indicating that Les Dawson's notion of the north was itself embedded in fading values. (On a personal note, after living in the north for forty years, I don't think I know a single person who eats black puddings and have never even seen tripe and cowheel pie. Not even in Rochdale.)

Les Dawson's departure from Yorkshire Television ushered in a curious and frenetic period which saw him sign to the BBC and embark on a run that pushed him ever closer to overexposure. Even a successful break in Hong Kong – to this day *Sez Les* and *The Les Dawson Show* are regularly screened there – couldn't help keep Dawson from

When You're Smiling

Les and Mother-in-law, Ada Plant. A loving scene

Under Attack

our screens. In 1977 he was still everywhere on telly. Most famously, and most enchantingly, he was seen chatting on the sets of Des O'Connor's and Michael Parkinson's chat shows and enriching the gaudy downbeat *Summertime Special* variety show filmed at Great Yarmouth for the BBC. This, perhaps, was a mistake, as it gave off signals of Dawson amid British seaside revelry, candyfloss and hot dogs, of a 1950s pastel seafront, precariously close to the archaic image that would continue to taint anything remotely 'end of pier'.

Opinion varies but perhaps the unjustified image of a northern prom strutter, gorging on fish'n'chips, wasn't quite what British comedy needed during the era when, for instance, British music had been thoroughly overhauled by the scream of punk and the sheer vivacity of disco. The prevailing atmosphere was one of change. The problem was, that although a few short years later there was a huge influx of new British comic talent, 1977 was strangely bereft of any noticeable comedic revolution.

That said, the BBC's *Les Dawson Show*, arguably the slickest series of his career, failed to set the ratings ablaze. My feeling is that, although containing some blistering poetic material, it relied too heavily on a tried-and-tested format, scurrying back to maintain a solid viewer-base rather than risking innovation. Les Dawson knew this was a wrong move. Unlike many comics in his situation, he had a talent for breaking new ground. In 1978 *The Dawson Watch* fared better. This was entirely the opposite to the dusty and reactionary *Les Dawson Show*. The talent, the delivery, the flow of wordplay remained, although this time it was presented from a set designed like a giant computer patrolled by beautiful girls. Although Dawson and producer Peter Whitmore awaited series transmission with a certain trepidation. *The Les Dawson Show* slowed the comic's progress. Could *The Dawson Watch* end it altogether? To their delight, and perhaps astonishment, *The Dawson Watch* garnered lively press notices and, for the first time, gathered considerable acreage in the broadsheets. Appealing to a more intellectual audience, Les Dawson found himself in the unlikely position of being hip! (Triggering a cult aspect to his appeal which remains intact to this day.) It was an incredible coup, rather like a goal scored in extra time, just as the crowd had started to disperse, just as the critics had been preparing for the final act of savagery. It was no accident that, as the flamboyant early 1980s exploded in a mass of colour and dreadful fashion, most 1970s comedians faded in an instant, condemned to end-of-the-pier obscurity. Dawson wasn't alone in surviving, but those who did crash that barrier earned a special kind of reverence.

When You're Smiling

And then came the bombshell. As Dawson found himself fired by career optimism once more, Meg was diagnosed with breast cancer. His new dual existence, attempting to balance personal tragedy while forging ahead with his comedy act, was a precarious balance and one which captured the public's heart, establishing a link between audience and comic that would later be seen as unique.

There followed a lengthy period of silence. Half a year passed before Dawson's face made another welcome appearance in our living rooms, as the sardonic new host of *Blankety Blank*. It was a relief, a relaxation even, for Dawson, who could swap banter with some of the sharpest minds of television with unnerving ease. There was a deceptive simplicity to the programme, and that ragged self-deprecating theme, originally set by Terry Wogan, lingered on. The televisual trick was to make the entire thing appear as an entertaining failure, as the pathetic anti-game show, with jokes falling flatly to the floor, with yawning guests and daffy egocentric guest celebs. The reality was rather different. To appear relaxed, disdainful even, while keeping such live-wire personalities as Lionel Blair and Keith Chegwin at bay, was a feat in itself.

1985

Life had twisted sourly for both Les and Meg. She was now in constant pain from cancer of the spine, a form that can take hold before anything untoward is noticed. Les was in recovery from a terrifying brush with death. He had been diagnosed with, and operated on for, cancer of the prostate gland, at a Preston hospital. Both patients wallowed in the black comedy of the situation as their eldest daughter, Julie – now a nurse – eased them back into something approaching normal life. Les Dawson's recovery was surprisingly swift. He joked in his autobiography that his improvement would have been much to the chagrin of the reporters who had been hovering around the hospital during his illness, cynically waiting for news of the latest comic death. It was one of the least funny jokes ever to spill from his pen, for it was too close to home.

A comedy death makes a sensational, dramatic story, capturing the attention of the readers and selling copies by the truck load. Had Les Dawson known the turmoil the

Opposite: Ecstasy by the sea

Under Attack

When You're Smiling

Les swapping black pudding recipes with Prince Philip

tabloid newspapers would plunge him into during the coming years, he would have had the scribblers removed from the hospital corridors. As it was, he let them be. It was part of the price of fame.

He would also refer to himself during this period as 'skeletal'. This has to be the exaggeration of the century, for one could imagine no such thing of Les. If he had lost weight, then it could be put down to the illness. He had to put weight back on, to build his strength up. He had to work again – if only to keep the Inland Revenue at bay. Financially, Les Dawson was lurching from one show to the next, managing to fight the wolves back from the door, but only just. Any break in that routine, be it from illness or for extended holidays, merely seemed to nudge him closer to debt. He had to get back to work but, before that, he had to take Meg to Manchester's world-renowned Christie's Hospital. The news wasn't good. But Meg's subsequent courageous and very public fight would prove inspirational.

*   *   *

Under Attack

Les and Meg

83

Chapter Seven

The Light And The Dark

IT IS DIFFICULT AND PERHAPS IMPOSSIBLE TO IMAGINE LES DAWSON IN AMERICA.

It might be too cosy, to think of him jabbering around a table with a motley assortment of Blackpool landladies or wandering along that unholy prom, soaking up the absurdities, honing his act. But how would such a talent respond to the multitudinous absurdities that America had to offer? Would he cope with America's overt and often cloying cheerfulness? How could he be so hilariously maudlin in such a climate? And, conversely, how would America react to Les? How could audiences possibly know how to respond to his self-deprecation when self-deprecation isn't part of their language?

One thinks of American comedians with a similar approach. There are, strangely enough, a number of not immediately apparent similarities between Les and the great Woody Allen. Both comics dredge their own insecurities and tend to connect with people who suffer similar mental pains. Physically speaking, Dawson might be seen as quite the antithesis of the weakling Allen. However, as both lived on the edge of accepted human physicality, albeit on opposite edges, their insecurities were strikingly similar. Of course, Allen never managed to achieve the success he deserved in his homeland, though he typified America in the eyes of Europeans. As Allen himself would admit, 'I'm basically a downbeat guy. And Americans don't like to admit that such a thing exists.'

With that in mind, what would America make of Les Dawson? Well, it has to be admitted that Les Dawson's brief foray to the States wasn't exactly on the scale of The Beatles. He wasn't given the opportunity to shake American humour to its foundations, mesmerising audiences from coast to coast, with his tales of truffle-eating basset hounds

Replacing the Irish – with a northern –. Les follows Terry

When You're Smiling

The king and queen of British gameshows: Les with Larry Grayson

and Lancashire life. It was 1985 and, fresh from finishing his novel *A Time Before Genesis*, and immediately prior to a spell in pantomime absurdity with the Manchester-based *Babes In The Wood*, Dawson was offered the chance to appear in a cabaret spot in the Westbury Hotel, on New York's plush Madison Avenue. It was, to say the least, a bizarre booking and Dawson, casting his mind back to some of the venues he had suffered in during his early career couldn't find the resolve to turn such an offer down. It was a pity, as the extra pressure was an unwelcome addition to an already exhausting workload. Meg, although very ill, encouraged him to go, knowing that he would always regret it if he missed the opportunity. It might even be a bit of a holiday. Which it must have

The Light And The Dark

seemed like to Les – in *No Tears For The Clown*, his second autobiographical volume, he spoke fondly of being served Dom Perignon by gorgeous stewardesses whilst zipping across the Atlantic on Concorde. It was, in part, a tourist trip, with Les bumbling through Manhattan like the archetypal Brit abroad, crashing through social barriers with all the impudence afforded the naïve traveller.

However, there was no escaping the horror to come. He was to perform in the soft-lit splendour of American top-bracket cabaret. A fascinating though nauseating arena, where ageing stars rattle out ancient hits, plying nostalgia to greying captains of industry and their bejewelled wives. Had Les Dawson's fame really penetrated such an alien environment? Actually, no. It transpired that the wife of the hotel owner, a Yorkshire woman, had expressed a desire to see Les perform. This was America. Such things happen over there. Personally, I would pay a reasonable amount of money to see a video of Dawson's performance that night. A performance, naturally, tempered and softened for American ears. Nevertheless, Dawson's surrealism floated way above the heads of the bemused crowds; how could he have known that in America muffins, the subject of one of his quickfire lines, were currant sponge cakes rather than the solid lumps of dough we know? The laughs were sparse, though not non-existent. There were enough fun-loving Brits in attendance to carry the whole thing through to the rousing out-of-tune piano finale and some things, it seems, share a universal language. That said, there were still some Americans who couldn't quite grasp the subtleties of our Les: 'He's interesting, but he sure needs a few piano lessons,' being a common review of his performance.

This period, the American jaunt followed by the extensive run in *Babes In The Wood*, famously highlighted the bitter-sweet nature of Dawson's life. The sheer thrill and frivolity of the panto, in which Dawson forged a loose working relationship with John 'Bergerac' Nettles, provided a welcome change from the pressures of TV stardom. One of the mysterious attractions of pantomime is the glory of seeing fine and distinguished actors willingly stoop to the kind of script level once attained by *Crackerjack*. The best performers, however, manage to build from the skeletal script, adding comic flurries here and there, keeping the whole show feeling fresh. No pantomime should ever trip along in a perfectly-scripted manner. It should stumble and fail, props and scenery should crash to the floor and the actors should back-pedal furiously, ad libbing, finding new and unexpected laughs, working the audience. It looks easy, of course, yet it is anything but. People who know about such things regard the Dawson/Nettles partnership, and indeed the entire *Babes In The Wood* Manchester show, as a classic (it was so good that it kept being revived in successive seasons with the same cast). The relationship between Dawson, as the fearsome Nurse Ada and Nettles as the Sheriff of Nottingham became a solid reference point in panto's curious folklore. Their twisting of the script received rave reviews and represented a triumph of talent and steely professionalism. The rest of the cast, unable to rely on the the safety of an adhered-to script were forced into a fluid performance. It all added an extra edge to the panto. Such things are regarded very seriously in the showbiz world, if nowhere else.

But Dawson's delight – one critic called him the finest pantomime dame of the century – was tempered by the rapidly deteriorating health of Meg, whose cancer had spread to the extent that the doctors at Christie's Hospital reluctantly informed an anguished Dawson that she perhaps only had a few weeks to live. The trauma of this period is best told by Les himself, within the pages of *No Tears For The Clown*. His personal battle, with God, with the afterlife, with the kind of spiritual meaning he had explored in his fiction, took on a profound new significance. His extraordinary work rate slowed to a crawl as he started to care for Meg – as well as taking on board increasingly large amounts of alcohol.

Meg's eventual and merciful death, on 15 April 1986, left Les in charge of the children. The responsibility was to be the making of him, especially as he also had to contend with a torrent of patronising tabloid press. Never one to suffer the worst excesses of the tabloids, Dawson retreated from the spotlight. For once, his open friendship with the people of St Annes was returned with interest, the locals keeping a respectful distance and giving short shrift to the tabloid writers who lurked awhile.

Still locked in a haze of misery over the death of his beloved Meg, Les found himself returning more and more to the bar of the St Ives Hotel, his favourite friendly haunt in Lytham. Here, through a wave of melancholia and alcohol, he swiftly fell in love with the beautiful barmaid who generously listened to his outpourings of grief.

The affair and subsequent marriage between Les and Tracy became the source of intense tabloid frenzy. The frenzy was so intense that the couple decided to confront the media attention, talking to selected reporters and appearing on television – *Good Morning With Anne And Nick* would eventually prove to be a particular favourite. Their regular cheerful appearances would connect naturally with the viewers, rendering tabloid speculation redundant.

The Light And The Dark

Let the anecdotes flow

When You're Smiling

Tracy and Les in holiday mood

The Light And The Dark

But that was in the future and Les and Tracy had many battles to face before they were accepted by press and public. It was some time before they even admitted their feelings to each other. Les fell for Tracy first, although he refused to admit to himself that such a beautiful person might find an ageing comic, rotund of frame and craggy of feature, remotely interesting.

There were other complications. Tracy was married and Les was looking after his three children. His emotional state was precarious. A friendship, spiced with an emotion that neither party wished to admit, seemed to be the only possible course to follow.

Whatever plans Les might have been making at the time were truly scuppered, in the nicest possible way, by the unexpected success of *Babes In The Wood*, which now beckoned for a season in Birmingham. The schedule was ferocious. Fourteen long weeks, two shows a day, a constantly evolving diet of ad lib. The Manchester success served only to increase the pressure. It had been dubbed 'Britain's finest panto' by more than one esteemed critic. That was an awful lot to live up to. The show had to remain fresh, on the very edge of anarchy. It had to retain a modern streak, too. The work was intense for everyone involved. All the more reason, of course, to relax in the after-show bar, with a few rounds. How else do actors quell the afterglow of performance? The buzz needs to be stifled, and Les was only too happy to let the alcohol do the job.

For Les Dawson, more so than for any of the other cast members, the work didn't begin and end with the pantomime. Far from it. Promotional duties beckoned constantly. He wrote too, slamming one-liners into his word processor, building a book, or an act or merely a collage of notes. It was all the same, really. The Les way: take a chunk of each day, even the difficult, emotional parts, twist them into comedy, capture them with commanding phrases, each perfectly suited to his dry delivery. This was the heart of Les's art. He was a writer, first and foremost. Even the pain he was feeling about Meg and the guilt he suffered because of his feelings for Tracy surfaced, somewhere, in his work, adding emotional resonance to the material. And that was part of the reason, of course, why everyone loved Les Dawson.

Far from being trapped by provincial panto, Les's image was all over the country at the time. On advertising billboards, on *Blankety Blank* re-runs, endlessly on the radio. Once again buried in work, his emotional life was pushed to the rear, only surfacing, as his autobiography explained, in fleeting phone calls to Tracy. In April he was back on *Blankety Blank*, which he had now started to edge further into the surreal. It was a curious

When You're Smiling

shift. It's interesting to note that, years later, Vic Reeves would cite the latter series of *Blankety Blank* as one of his main inspirations for *Big Night Out*. The comparison may not seem immediately apparent. But Reeves had always been a big fan of Dawson. And wouldn't it be interesting, he once noted, if Dawson's intelligent surrealism were allowed to flourish in a peak-time light entertainment programme? The rise of Vic 'n' Bob from obscure surrealists to a position where they can appear on prime-time TV, is a similar success story to that of Les Dawson. One likes to think that Les would have heartily approved of *Families At War*. It's certainly difficult to watch without acknowledging the debt it owes to Dawson-period *Blankety Blank*.

An appearance at the Howard Keel Golf Classic Dinner with Tracy by his side was all that was needed to propel Les Dawson and his new girl into the headlines. Although, at the time, this media focus seemed savage, especially to Tracy, it can in retrospect be seen as a backhanded compliment. The tabloids knew full well that the name 'Les Dawson' was an instant hit with their readership. Les would, of course, despise them with an understandable fervour, but perhaps he should have seen the compliment in the headlines. That said, the doorstepping which ensued after the Howard Keel dinner – now officially recognised as Les and Tracy's 'coming out' ball – must have been terrible to endure. Imagine striding through St Anne's, with a reporter rushing by your side, constantly asking: 'Les, Les, Les, who is she? Les, Les, who is she?' It was worse than that. The absurdity of 1980s Britain was beginning to bite. Cars tailed him across the Pennines. Dictaphones were slipped next to ash trays on bars where his elbows rested. For all I know, his phone might have been bugged. And why? Because he, a lonely widower who had plumbed the depths of despair, had found a little happiness? Is that such a ground-breaking shock-horror tale? One only had to take a tiny step back to see the absurdity in this non-story. And yet, there was Les, as photogenic as an angry rhino, on the front pages, arm in arm with a beautiful young girl. In PR terms it was a disaster. Rarely can such a common tale of love been presented in such a sordid manner. Although one can understand the reason the reporters ran the story, it was also easy to see how such a precarious emotional situation was grossly exploited.

They coped, but only just. Tabloid hacks recorded their every move until, eventually, the couple allowed one of the reporters they both trusted, Hillary Bonner of the *Daily Mirror*, an exclusive, in order to kill the story. It was the start of a PR battle, in which Les and Tracy would only communicate on their own terms, through journalists they trusted.

The Light And The Dark

As a long-term strategy, this worked so well that the pair gained a certain infamy, even respect, among the tabloids. Had they capitulated in the face of that initial onslaught, their growing affection for each other might have crumbled. Even Les, used to such pressures, would surely have found the situation unbearable.

But there were positive aspects. The groundswell of support in and around Lytham St Annes grew and grew. Once Les and Tracy, by now living together, were courageous enough to go about their daily business, be it shopping at the local Safeway, or strolling among the dunes, they were astounded by the unequivocal approval of the locals. Even in the mail box, where a few 'nasties' did flop, the majority of letters were overwhelmingly positive. What happened, and one senses that even Les never quite grasped this, was that the couple were cushioned by the vast well of affection built up during his years of television exposure. It was not a patronising affection, nor was it steeped in blind fan adoration. Indeed, the reverse may be said. Through his work, Les Dawson believed in and encouraged the intelligence of everyday people. Somehow they understood this, and held no resentment towards his fame or the way he lived his life.

The period had its farcical touches, sometimes literally. In the glare of press exposure, Les had been appearing in the touring *Run For Your Wife*, a heady and clever little romp revolving around themes of infidelity, press intrusions and marital strife. He was not unaware of the irony in this situation. The only course of action open for Dawson's lively mind was to slip in ad libs turning his own difficult circumstances into comedy. That, of course, was his genius. It won over audiences and banished the weird atmosphere that had started to creep into the theatres they played. It also freed the rest of the cast, who grasped the jokes and took the play on to a new level of irony. How extraordinary to find Les once again relying on sheer force of talent to escape a predicament.

The 1987 *Royal Variety Performance*, Dawson's seventh on the trot, was a pivotal affair, striking a balance between the old guard – James Galway, Johnny Ray, Les Dawson – and the new, or newish, Ben Elton, Hale And Pace, Rik Mayall and others. In later years it would be regarded as the opening of the flood gates for a torrent of new comedy talent including Steve Coogan, Caroline Aherne and Dawson aficionados Vic 'n' Bob. The downside of this new swell of original talent would be the death of the word 'variety'. (Although Reeves and Mortimer would later attempt to revive the concept.) As such, in 1987, the factions in British entertainment were at war, and the *Royal Variety Performance* had taken on a distinctively reactionary flavour. Out of style, perhaps – certainly it

When You're Smiling

couldn't command anything like the television figures of its heyday, although competition was considerably stronger – the bill fought to retain some kind of old guard dignity. (Rosemary Clooney? Mel Torme?) But that year's show was particularly memorable for the way all these inner showbiz tensions crumbled in the face of one act to the extent that debates about the old and the new seemed, well, ludicrous. The act, of course, was Les Dawson, lumpy-faced, downbeat and famously supported by The Roly Polys, who, despite a few initial critical objections, turned in their most memorable performance. It was difficult to know what to say, after witnessing such a spectacle.

It was regarded as a victory for the old guard. Nobody, however, was fooled by this and one critic perceptively noted that 'Dawson's brilliance was like a last brave attack from an art form rapidly becoming archaic.'

It had taken longer than anyone expected – five long years had passed since the first series of *The Young Ones* announced a new era for comedy and Ben Elton's influence had seeped into so many areas of light entertainment – but the walls were now crumbling rapidly. A younger audience were demanding barbed topicality, hard-edged satire and even toilet humour. The Edinburgh Festival and its tight little fringe were now seen as feeder schools for the television companies. And, indeed, the television production teams were now staffed, almost entirely it seemed, by bedenimed youngsters, hungry to catch the new wave. Television comedy and, indeed, stand-up revue, had found its own equivalent to punk. *The Royal Variety Show* was regarded as little more than a quaint throwback. Even stubble-chinned pseudo-poets were clambering onto the scene, offering their dreadful politico rants, catching the attention of *Guardian* editors. In many ways the new revolution was wildly exciting, even if it had unfolded very slowly. Many old guard comedians had long ago submitted to the demands of television, and were now merely running through the motions, on dreadful quiz shows or hiding out in pantomime land.

Les Dawson, now engaged to Tracy and happier than he had been for years, had fallen off the pace. Unlike some of his peers – who would slide to end of pier obscurity in Cromer – he at least recognised the change in the climate. Television work, in particular, was offering fewer possibilities although the evergreen *Blankety Blank* kept him in the glare of prime time. Dangerously, perhaps, he opted for what he believed would be the safety of a summer season at Blackpool Opera House where, surrounded by an army of his fans, he could survive in a pocket of adoration.

The Light And The Dark

Not Les' idea of a fish supper

When You're Smiling

But even in Les Dawson's favourite town, where showbiz trends tend to linger for aeons, there was a sense that a large, traditional variety bill had become archaic. More successful, it seemed, were the productions, that had finally fallen from the top of the West End box office list, like *Cats* and *Joseph*. This time around, a bill topped by Les Dawson and featuring the immense local draws of Frank Carson, Keith Harris And Orville and, of course, The Roly Polys, wouldn't be enough to pull the crowds. It still appealed, but mainly to the disappearing army of traditional Blackpool holidayers, who were more and more opting for Spanish sunshine. In their place came a new breed of holidaying animal – a wild, rampant young hedonist, surging from bar to bar, dancing in chrome and neon discos. Blackpool's own revolution was under way and, while it hardly mirrored the new fashionability of the comedy scene, there was the sense of an invasion by a younger crowd who needed far more than a nightly slap of good old showbiz.

What's more, Les Dawson knew it. The audience response had been excellent, but they were an audience thin at the edges. Sensing blood, the critics weighed heavily in, castigating the show as 'old hat'. The problem with the press, this time around, was rather different. They were justified in their condemnation and Les Dawson, never one to suffer from self-disillusionment, knew it. Things would have to change, and change quickly.

> Tracy: 'Les always had a lot of time for people. If he was working at the theatre and there would be a young comic in the show, he would leave the dressing room door open and say, "I heard that gag today. Why don't you try it this way?" He always had time and he shared a lot. He always remembered how hard it was for him coming up in the business. I think in all walks of life he had a lot of compassion. I think that's why he was so loved and liked.'

Jim Casey: 'The only thing I ever knew that made Les angry was if someone was talking down to somebody else and was being big-headed, or in some way attacking someone who couldn't defend themselves. Like a big star having a go at a smaller act. Now, that would make him very angry and he would really have a go at them.

'We used to record two shows at a time and normally we would start at half-past twelve, have a break for lunch and then carry on rehearsing until 7pm. But in order to cut down the possible drinking time for Les, we finished up meeting at 4pm, to rehearse two shows and then do them at 8pm. But he still managed to get to the bar at 7pm.

He'd come out at five-past eight and would walk around the circle and heckle me when I was doing the warm-up. The thing is that the drink never seemed to affect his performance. Maybe it helped.'

It was a difficult spell, swiftly truncated by a heart attack. While Dawson lay like a curmudgeonly beached whale in South Fylde Hospital, his place was taken by The Krankies. I cannot for the life of me understand why anyone would wish to watch The Krankies, but they did and, perhaps to Dawson's chagrin, attendances started to creep back up. There is, of course, no accounting for taste and The Krankies, with their slightly cult appeal, seemed to sit better with a younger crowd. For Dawson, the battle was now just distant thunder. Ordered to relax, his temper merely simmered as he saw Ben Elton and the gang spill on to prime-time chat shows everywhere. For a while Les Dawson stopped watching the television altogether.

His recovery was steady, and softened by the odd part working sea cruises – on the *Canberra* for example – where too often he found himself floating to the bar. Nevertheless, it was a quiet, not altogether disagreeable spell, which saw Les and Tracy moving towards their hugely publicised wedding, part-financed by a hastily arranged Ford commercial. Dawson's name, and his link with potential purchasers, was still cherished in the advertising industry.

The period was perfectly timed, as it eased Dawson through a fairly difficult recovery. Honeymooning in a Scottish castle settled his anxiety and the good news that he was to host the revamped *Opportunity Knocks* seemed to calm his fears about having evolved into an outmoded art form.

But as Ben Elton was to note on the 1988 Radio Four show *Price of Laughter*: 'There were huge changes in the television industry and in people's perception of humour at that point. We all knew that things would never be the same again and a few faces simply faded away. But there are some people who are simply beyond trends. If you are a unique performer you transcend such changes. I never had any doubt that the very best, the funniest people on television would survive, and indeed come back stronger. And that's how it proved, with continued success for people like Bob Monkhouse, Bruce Forsyth and Les Dawson. People inside television thought that these people would be swept away but, in that sense, it was a false dawn because nothing new came along that was even comparable to them.'

With the new *Opportunity Knocks* on the horizon and with another batch of *Blankety*

When You're Smiling

Blanks in the can, reports of Dawson's demise certainly appeared to be premature. And when the summer of 1990, was blessed with the offer of an eight-week revue in the Festival Theatre, Paignton, the only immediate worry was, once again, of overwork. For once, Lady Luck was on Les Dawson's side. The house that Les and Tracy rented in Paignton came equipped with a swimming pool – perfect for a summer blessed with an unlikely run of hot weather. It was a fairly calm spell and, despite the still dwindling crowds – it was too hot to cram into a theatre – the season seemed refreshingly free from the kind of pressures apparent at Blackpool a year earlier. By comparison, Paignton and Torquay seemed relaxed. The on-stage atmosphere was rippled only by the delicate fact that Dawson's co star, Dana, was rather more heavily pregnant than expected. This fact proved difficult to hide and, again, Dawson used the situation to his comedic advantage.

Television stations work in mysterious ways. Ideas are bounced around endless meetings attended by a myriad of people whose actual jobs defy description. Far more often than not, the ideas end up in the bin. Above this level, however, is another where ideas actually stem from people with a little power, and can often result in a project getting a small working budget. Even so, they usually finish up spiked for rejected. A few, however, do get through. Then there is the top layer: established producers pushing archaic ideas across safe prime-time fodder. At this level, programmes actually do get made, which is an incredible and rare thing. Contrary to popular belief, television trends change very slowly. At least, they did in 1990, before the satellite and cable revolution.

*   *   *

The Light And The Dark

Despite the similarities with WC Fields, Les didn't make it Stateside

Chapter Eight

Embracing The New Wave

THE AGE OF VARIETY, THE COUNTRY HAD DECIDED, WAS OVER.

Les Dawson, an intelligent and versatile talent, would surely have benefited, at this point, from a influx of young, creative programming. However, the BBC chose instead to offer him a short series of Les Dawson shows. With this, in addition to his *Blankety Blank* commitments, Dawson's year was suddenly beginning to swell with work. With typical irony, this latter-day series of *Les Dawson* was probably one of the finest, blessed with guests including Status Quo, Shirley Bassey and David Essex. However, as that list strongly indicates, it was a show completely out of time. Indeed, much to Dawson's continuing anxiety, the BBC chose to run the show simultaneously with *Blankety Blank* which, coincidentally, had also started to slip. The ironies pile up here. Most television entertainers, during their later days, slip into a parody of their former selves. Dawson was still sharp, still capable of commanding attention, even from younger viewers. Yet the powers that be, in television or elsewhere, seemed only to be able to see Les within the same old format. Although the series gained numerous positive reviews, it still seemed noticeably dated. Dawson himself said: 'It was so out of date they should have filmed it on flick-books.'

A spell in a lukewarm pantomime in Sunderland hardly improved the situation. The problem was that the audience was turning away from the show's format, although not from Les. The public still felt a great deal of affection for Dawson and, for the most part, were wholly unaware that any kind of career crisis was taking place. After all, he was still on their screens. They neither knew nor cared that panic within the television and entertainment industries accelerates via a kind of domino effect, as everybody backs

Despite his success, Les often suffered pre-show doubts

When You're Smiling

After the show, he'd inevitably relax with a gurn and a glass

Embracing The New Wave

swiftly away from anything or anyone rumoured to be on the way down. What was needed was a new format based around the familiar figure of Dawson.

The decision to shift Dawson into a revived version of *Opportunity Knocks* seems bizarre, to say the least. Of all the shows in all the world guaranteed to cling like bindweed to its host, *Opportunity Knocks* takes the biscuit. It was, and still is, utterly impossible to hear the world *Opportunity Knocks* without your mind becoming instantly graced by the sight of Hughie Green and his stunningly patronising catchphrase: 'Annnd I meeeen thaaaat moast sincerely, folks!'

Opportunity Knocks was Hughie Green's baby. It was Green who pioneered the format as a radio show for several years before coming up with the idea of a viewer-participation programme, complete with the astounding clapometer and the weekly array of hapless would-be stars. The BBC would eventually attempt to finally expunge Green from the series when they re-titled the show after Les's tenure as host had ended; *Bob Says Opportunity Knocks* ushered Bob Monkhouse into the hot seat as host, but it was still not enough to eradicate the memory of Hughie Green.

A sizeable budget was expertly used to provide the new series with an up-beat, modern feel. A good setting, perhaps, for Dawson to weave his idiosyncratic surrealism into this ancient warhorse. He worked hard at it, too, fuelled by a genuine belief that a door should always be left open for new talent to parade before the television camera. After all, this was the format in which he first attracted attention. Again, although the ratings were not huge, there was a strange gulf between the feelings of Dawson's genuine followers and the critics who, fired by the rush of new generation comedy, savagely attacked anything that was not young and subversive. One might argue that exposing new talent in the public arena was itself innovative, but the critics couldn't grasp that notion at all. *Opportunity Knocks* was slammed from all angles. The format was too old. Or the format had been changed too much. Dawson wasn't allowed to be himself on the show. Or his presence was too intrusive.

The only comfort in all this was that the criticisms were profoundly inconsistent. The show couldn't be all these things at once. The only constant was a full-blooded attack on Dawson. Confused more than dispirited, Dawson spent time fluttering around as a guest on various television chat shows. This was a positive step, at least. Although it hardly earned Dawson much money, it did allow him to put his point of view across. No critic seeking to destroy the old guard could silence Dawson, even though many tried and just

When You're Smiling

as many failed. It was an uneven contest. Dawson only had to pull a face to be able to render any serious attack redundant. And, as Michael Parkinson pointed out, 'If you are asking Les a serious question and, half-way through it his face breaks into something resembling a sack of spuds – how on Earth do you manage to get your point across? The thing is, you can't, because he just dissolves everything.'

Dawson's disarming fizzog ensured that clips of his time spent as interviewee, intended to promote his books, would constantly resurface in the 'Best of British Comedy' clips that would be repeated every Christmas. The importance of these clips wouldn't become apparent for some time. Years later, they would seem extraordinary when the merest flicker of his deadpan scowl would send intelligent people into fits of mirth. For those whose television watching began after the Dawson era, this would remain utterly bewildering. The sight of a plump face, wrinkled and leery, burbling out streams of bewildering gibberish would prove baffling. But then they would listen a little bit more. And they, too, would pluck odd phrases from the monologues – and soon Dawson's anarchic sense of humour would infect a new generation of aficionados.

He had become a living cult, with new members joining daily. He was ambitious enough to claw his way on to television and yet he seemed to be offering something more, seeking something other than mere gratification. I am not suggesting there wasn't a huge ego at work behind that cratered moon of a face, but this was a man so obviously attempting to communicate, someone on the side of the underdog. It was a different kind of genius. You may admire the quick-fire super-corn of Bob Monkhouse, or the sheer arrogant gall of Bruce Forsyth, or even the sheer force of the brogue gushing from Frank Carson, but would you want to get drunk with any of these people? One always sensed that, should you ever attempt such a thing, in some soft-lit showbiz bar, you would be drowned in a sea of self-obsessed gush.

With Dawson, your drunken conversation could swing two ways, but you would feel sure that Les would be interested in you! Because he *was* interested in you. Even if, perhaps especially if, you were a scone-scoffing grannie escaped from a Rochdale housing estate and briefly ensconced in a Blackpool guest house decorated after the school of Hilda Ogden.

At this point, Dawson's career seemed to be in terminal decline. And then, just as he was about to land belly down in the knacker's yard of showbiz has-beens, a funny thing happened. For reasons only known to himself, He spilled his heart out to a passing

Embracing The New Wave

Les as a great panto dame

When You're Smiling

Cissie and Ada, posing

tabloid hack who, for once – isn't this just bloody typical? – wrote the article accurately. No fabrication needed here: this was a television personality falling from grace. Nobody wanted him. Nobody loved him. He was careering head-first into obscurity!

Except that he wasn't. You can rely on Manchester, if nowhere else, to produce the unexpected. When the article appeared, just at the moment when the public might start feeling sorry for such a has-been, the advance booking for his forthcoming pantomime at Manchester's Palace Theatre broke all known records. I actually have first-hand experience of this, as I was working for the *Manchester Evening News* at the time and, I freely admit, was writing critically against the notion of pantomimes and found myself in an altercation with people at the Palace who informed me of this statistic. I checked it out, and it was true. This didn't sadden me, for Dawson was a hero of sorts, but it really did surprise me. Hadn't the world moved on? Wasn't all this stuff outmoded?

Embracing The New Wave

Theatre entrepreneur Larry Price: 'A strange thing happened in the early 1990s. Not across the board, but certainly with a few of the leading comedians. The people who had been all-but wiped away by all the alternative comedy stuff suddenly started coming back. There was a real surge in demand for the better people. I think there was a reactionary thing, people had seen and heard the new stuff, perhaps liked some of it and disliked a lot of it, and started to demand to see people like Les again. And that's why people like Bob Monkhouse came back stronger than ever. People were told that they had gone for good and the audiences wouldn't have it. It was a marvellous turnaround.'

Turnaround indeed. Suddenly Dawson, along with a flu-ridden John Nettles and Anne Sydney and The Roly Polys, pushed hoary old panto *Babes In The Wood* to a new peak. For Manchester, it was extraordinary. Les was suddenly in demand. His name was all over local diary and gossip columns. In the *Manchester Evening News* there was even a Les Dawson fashion spread, if you can believe such a thing. Ten weeks sped by with the cast, meeting nightly in the bar, fired by the enthusiasm of an unexpected success. And all this despite Les's horrendous health problems. One of the true panto 'downers' is that the children who cram into the theatre daily bring an alarming variety of germs with them, feisty little bugs that could easily undermine the precarious health of an overweight lead actor with a fondness for alcohol.

Alas, Dawson's glorious panto triumph would be crushed by the BBC's decision to produce a downmarket game show, heavily reminiscent of the kind of 'swift buck' shows notorious on the American television market. The BBC – correctly, as it turned out – assumed that the future of light entertainment belonged to crass formats, crazed and sad guests, cheesy egocentric hosts and sets that would have disgraced the average travelling funfair. But somewhere, deep in the foggy heart of the Beeb's most curious hierarchy, the decision to make a crass game-show called *Fast Friends* was made. The show centred around contestants willing to suffer the most profound embarrassments, and say or do anything to get their faces on TV. The point of the show was to exploit the naiveté of the contestants. It was crass, cheap television. Fortunately for all involved the rules of the game proved too complex for either the contestants or, he admitted, the host to understand. Les didn't want to do the show. His agents, Norman Murray and Anne Chudleigh, were against it. But the Beeb's bizarre interest in using Dawson as host persisted – and they got their man.

Why Dawson? The BBC had seen him ride the lull in fortunes. They believed him to

When You're Smiling

be able to add a particular Englishness to proceedings. They thought his familiarity would soften the show's brassy American style. Five years later it might have worked. As it stood, the show's aura of anarchy was more confusing than, say, the very British *Tiswas*. But here we had a string of contestants, all of whom seemed a little too familiar with people who regularly watch game-shows, attempting to wrestle the attention away from a curiously under-confident Dawson. *Fast Friends* was the complete antithesis of *Blankety Blank*, which was a veritable feast of English self-deprecation and beguiling pointlessness. But with *Blankety Blank*, despite its batch of celebrities, the focus was on Dawson at the end of every joke. On *Fast Friends*, he never really managed to take the reins. In *No Tears For The Clown*, Dawson hinted strongly that the on-screen chaos was more than matched by the squabbling backstage. Critically, of course, it was caned – deservedly so. The BBC completely missed the mark. The question was, how deeply would this affect Les Dawson's fragile self-confidence, let alone his position with the fickle general public? Dawson's career was beginning to rear and plunge like the roller-coaster at Blackpool Pleasure Beach. The only silver lining in view was the opportunity for him to concentrate on his family life.

What happened to Dawson next would not be believed outside the most absurdly disjointed script. Who would steal into the story and resurrect Dawson's career at this point? The answer for Les was simple. When in doubt, when the sycophants have fled and your name once again begins to surface in the past tense – send for Ada!

Wonderful, vivacious Ada, forever languishing in Cissie's slipstream. Back they both came into Dawson's life. Back to remind people why they loved Dawson in the first place: for reflecting their own absurdities. Cissie and Ada – still regarded as one of the great British comic creations of the age. Dawson and Barraclough found themselves back on TV together, although this time in cartoon form for a commercial for the Post Office. This gloriously ubiquitous and affectionate (if rather non-PC) ad was a send-up of housewives' street gossip. And it was the advert that gained a lively cult following for Cissie and Ada, which touched a nerve with the juvenile humour common to university social clubs. Cissie and Ada clubs sprang into action, at Warwick, Lancaster and elsewhere. Admittedly, they were on a par with the dubious 'I like Anne Diamond's Knickers' club of Cambridge, but nevertheless they were a compliment of sorts.

*   *   *

Embracing The New Wave

Les and Tracy on their big day

Chapter Nine

A Wonderful Life

LES DAWSON'S CULT APPEAL DEEPENED AND DARKENED WITH THE UNEXPECTED ARRIVAL OF LA NONA.

La Nona (in Spanish, 'The Old One') was an extraordinary social satire written by Roberto Crossa in which a one-hundred-year-old Argentine woman, beset by profound obesity, spends her day devouring everything that is laid before her by her hard-working family. She is a giant, gutless slob literally eating away at the heart of the family who fit in uncomplainingly around her. La Nona was a metaphor for the Argentine economy and the futility of her existence can be seen as a universal theme. At least, the BBC thought so when it decided to pluck *La Nona* from the Spanish-speaking world and remake it for British television audiences. BBC bosses must have been quaking with trepidation.

The choice of Les Dawson for the lead role was simply inspired. The physical reasons for this were obvious, but it would guarantee that a large section of the viewers would tune in, expecting an hour of surrealism and merriment. They weren't disappointed on the first count, but to see Dawson immersed in the utter bleakness of such a piece was shocking. The image of Dawson's *La Nona* would linger for years after the message of the play had been forgotten. If, indeed, the message had ever been accepted in the first place.

There is considerably doubt about this last point. In *No Tears For The Clown*, Dawson was angry and irritated with British journalists who attended the press screening and who seemed more concerned with his weight than the play itself. Whether the audience ever decided whether *La Nona* was anything more than a play about a fat woman who ate a lot – I cannot put my hand on my heart and say I saw anything beyond the play's physical absurdities – is a matter of serious doubt. It was, however, utterly intriguing to

Preparing for La Nona

When You're Smiling

Tracy, Les and (hiding) Charlotte

all who stumbled across it. Dawson, surrounded by a fearsome cast including Liz Smith, Maurice Denham, Timothy Snell and Jane Horrocks, certainly managed to dominate the screen. It was interesting, also, to note the slightly frosty dressing room meeting between a half-dressed Dawson and Horrocks who cheekily stated, 'Ooooh, I've never seen anyone so fat before!'

It was anything but an insult. Horrocks' intention was to break pre-rehearsal nerves and she fully expected Dawson to grasp the situation with his usual comic dexterity. For once, he missed his cue.

'I don't think he was very amused,' she admitted later.

La Nona greatly enhanced Dawson's status, setting him apart from those comics of his generation still in action. It was screened on BBC2 and garlanded with superlative reviews. Viewing figures did not scale the heights, but that didn't matter. The majority of the audience seemed to enjoy the sight of Les Dawson in such unusual surroundings.

Despite *La Nona*, and certainly not because of it, as one malicious critic noted, Dawson's television appearances were thinning noticeably. When he did appear, it was usually as a player on the endless book-plugging circuit. (His typically sardonic take on Raymond Chandler – *Well Fared, My Lovely* – added sprinklings of sheer daftness, as well as northern grit, and took Chandler's prose into a quite absurd new territory.) It may not have grasped the attention of Britain's book critics, but it provided a splendid opportunity for the publishers to organise lengthy publicity tours. When the author was Les Dawson, a crowd at each shop and listeners to every radio interview were guaranteed. The problem, at least as far as Les and Tracy were concerned, was that it meant a great deal of work and travel, with no immediate financial rewards.

To compensate, Dawson took the path favoured by many fading luminaries. He joined the after-dinner speaking set – in his case, not a bad idea, as hilarious monologues had been his forte for decades. Dawson could be trusted to transform his dour ramblings into sparkling, if surreal, repartee. Which he did, reducing the banqueting suites of luxurious London hotels such as the Royal Garden in Kensington, Grosvenor House and the Park Lane Hilton to a giggling heap of dishevelled blue-chip diners.

Throughout this period, one thing became obvious. In Lanky-speak, the snootier the do, the more they loved him. His unpretentious persona seemed to be welcomed into such affairs, almost as a relief, as an antidote to ceremony and stuffiness. Les Dawson swept away black-tie formality. With Les Dawson in your midst, pretension and

When You're Smiling

pomposity didn't stand much chance. He mercilessly lampooned these affairs and not once did he receive the faintest trace of complaint from his well-heeled audience.

It was hard work, however, and it brought its own brand of stress: not, perhaps, the kind of life perfectly suited to a man who seriously needed to slow down. He did slow down, though, while basing himself in London for these talks.

Another twist was waiting for him, one that would point Dawson towards his next unexpected triumph. Despite *La Nona*'s strange success, he was still depressed and still lacking confidence. This intensified the more he stared at the telephone. It's a showbiz axiom that the buzz of success is always matched by the anti-climax which follows. It usually strikes when the star sits at home, unable to cope with domestic life, waiting for the phone to ring. For Les Dawson, whose working-class fear of failure began to creep back up to him when his diary started to look free, the quiet spells were a nightmare.

> Tracy Dawson: 'He always used to think: "I'll just do this last pantomime, this last show, you never know, we might run out of money." He always felt the working-class side of things could come back tomorrow, that we could lose everything. "Yes, I'll just do that last show." But I don't think it would ever have really been his last show. He would have always worked.'

It was understandable paranoia. Dawson's childhood had instilled in him a profound work ethic where, after a couple of weeks mowing a lawn in Lytham, or wandering the parks of central London, he would be wracked with guilt. A massive irony, as the breathing space between his thinning television appearances was exactly what Les Dawson needed. Time to relax, time to write. He wasn't destitute. He still had a large and loyal following that extended way beyond those who had picked up on him through his hilarious performances on *Blankety Blank*. He worried, too much, about the younger, thinner, hipper comics, dishing out toilet humour, PC politico rants, the 1990s take on life. It is a real pity that Les Dawson couldn't sense there was longevity in his work. His agents knew it, but getting him to believe it was an impossible task.

Paranoia indeed. Enough to inspire him to turn down the *Royal Variety Performance* that year. The *Royal Variety* was already ageing fast. In a courageous effort to reverse its decline, that year's show was relatively modern. Yet this also produced fresh problems for Les and his precarious confidence. Diana Ross. Jackie Mason. David Frost.

A Wonderful Life

Les' final TV appearance; in Demob, *broadcast on 29 October 1993*

115

When You're Smiling

You've got the cutest little baby face…

Ned Sherrin. Wayne Sleep. OK, so it wasn't exactly a youthfest, but the names on display were serious showbiz talent. The name Les Dawson, of course, slipped effortlessly into this list. But that wasn't quite how Les saw it. Until, as he explained in his autobiography, he discovered that his appearance had been requested by old sparring partner Prince Philip. And Les Dawson could never resist the pull of royalty. To his agent's delight, to Tracy's delight, he said yes.

A Wonderful Life

While buoyed by the royal interest – royal insistence, perhaps – the bill still intimidated Dawson. His nervousness as the big day approached was later recalled in a variety of interviews. The interviews themselves were triumphant, following one of the most memorable performances of his career. Dawson was charismatic from his first risqué broadside to his absurd piano finale. Sandwiched between the two were a cluster of short, sharp, Dawsonisms. 'It's wonderful to be here in this marvellous old theatre, such an intimate atmosphere. It reminds me of home… it's filthy and full of strangers.'

I don't know why I was sitting in my front room, utterly engrossed by this, as I hadn't watched a *Royal Variety Show* in years, but this had been a curiously invigorating show. Perhaps a refreshing reactionary stab. A last stab, too, as the Eltons, Enfields and Mayalls would soon be swiftly followed by the Newmans and Baddiels, the Skinners, the Coogans and Ahernes, a whole new hierarchy taking their place.

We somehow seemed to sense this. But that inevitable comic revolution only intensified the enjoyment of this particular evening where the old guard – Eric Idle, once so impishly anarchic, latterly so sadly uninspiring – rediscovered at least some of their old shine. It was a collective encore and the most fantastic performance of the evening, was our Les. Perhaps it was a performance driven by his pent-up paranoia. Perhaps we, the viewers, simply ached for his familiar patter. No matter how hip we were, Dawson was a flashback to a television era where he stuck out as quality among the flotsam and jetsam of prime-time TV. He stole the show. Everybody knew it. That night, Les Dawson smiled as a well-earned alcoholic haze slowly crept across his features. He'd won: the odds were against him, but he'd won.

The press even acknowledged this, pulling Les Dawson straight back into the spotlight, if only because of a daft tale about Dawson and his television commercials for the Post Office, which involved Les being falsely accused of ranting at his local postman while fronting the campaign on TV. It was proven to be a complete fabrication, but that mattered little. It was a good angle and the rotund comic from Lytham had no chance against a tabloid attack. He could do little more than grimace and rely on no-nonsense St Annes to prove that the public supported him unreservedly.

Les and Tracy were deliriously happy in Lytham, although their time there was often brief. The panto season had a strange knack of beckoning just when they had settled into blissful home life. This time, it was *Dick Whittington* in Wimbledon, with John Nettles, Rula Lenska and The Roly Polys as the crew of the ship. Les's fortunes swung back in his favour again as the panto became a huge success. Seven weeks of crazed, uncontrollable screaming and ranting – and, as he no doubt told someone in a bar, the audiences were even worse. Success at Wimbledon was immediately followed by success at Leeds, the British city where Dawson's profile was perhaps at its highest, this despite a lifetime of casting aspersions on Yorkshire – 'Oh, I admit Yorkshire does exist, but who in their right mind would want to go to Ripon? Let Yorkshire act as ballast and thank the Lord for the Pennine chain.'

None of this 'roses' prejudice mattered a jot. They understood Les Dawson in Leeds. They accepted him in their pubs as if he was an ageing centre-half from their fearsome 1970s football team. Despite the fact that Dawson's most terrifying comic experiences always seemed to take place in Yorkshire clubs, the local historians inform us that Manchester comedy always connected with the beer-swilling social club members of Leeds, Bradford, Wakefield and Sheffield. It was 'northern' and that was good enough for most people. Strangely, the comic knack of levelling inter-city prejudice never worked in Liverpool which, despite being a mere 36 miles from Manchester, always existed on an entirely different cultural plane. Unlike many of his peers, Dawson could and did play Liverpool often, and even if the Mancunian vowels encouraged a certain unease in the crowd, they appreciated his surreal humour.

> Les Dawson: 'The average Liverpudlian possesses the uncanny ability of being able to put a string of improbable words together and in doing so produce a verbal painting. For instance, I was talking to a Scouser in a pub off Lime Street and I asked him if he was still living in The Dingle, which is a slum area of the city. His reply had me in hysterics. "Naw. We got rehoused in Kirkby. It's all right but de house is small. It's a real vampire's haystack." I adored that. I thought about that for weeks afterwards.'

Well, he would, wouldn't he? Vampire's haystack? Pure Dawsonian. Liverpudlian humour surges into a verbal world beyond the mundane. It's there all the time, in the skinny, spotty oiks who look after your car for 50p, in every pub and every front room. It's in *Brookside*, in Anfield and Goodison, in the Albert Dock and the Tate Gallery, from Speke to Maghull. That's not to endorse the tired myth that every living Scouser is a born comic, which is nonsense, but the prevailing language, shot through with visual imagery,

A Wonderful Life

Les, Tracy and Charlotte signing copies of No Tears For the Clown

When You're Smiling

Charlotte Dawson

seems curiously close to the idiosyncratic mutterings of Les Dawson. As Dawson would admit, on Radio Four's *Start The Week*:

> 'I understand Liverpool people, I understand Yorkshire people, too. I might poke fun at them both, but I poke fun at Mancunians, too. The funny thing is that a lot of the people in these cities believe they are so different from each other. I never saw that geographical divide. It's a nonsense and I like to think that a lot of the work I do transcends that, in all honesty. I'm prejudiced against people who are prejudiced. I don't like bullies, I never have. And there are just as many bullies in Manchester as there are in Liverpool. These are all struggling city people with an awful lot of problems. But they have also got immense potential, incredible skills, incredible intelligence. The only time I have doubted this is when they fight each other, but that's just a small minority, a few bad football fans and the like. And you get idiots everywhere. You get idiots in Surbiton. You get intelligent people in London. No, honestly, you do. I met one, once.'

Following *Dick Whittington* there was a particularly moving *This is Your Life*, during which Michael Aspel, with help from the Dawsons, presented the big red book to the leading Roly Poly, Mighty Mo Moreland. The programme was unusual in that it flattered the attendant celebrities in the normal fashion, but everyone who appeared seemed remarkably unaffected. It was a glimpse into the inner sanctum of Blackpool showbiz. Big of heart, bold as brass, honest and open. Egotistical, of course, but it was a noticeably warm and welcoming ego. Television critics in London offices dismissed the programme with one snide remark. One prominent London-based columnist, not noted for his liberal opinions, dismissed the participants as 'a gathering of horrendous northerners who had seemingly escaped from some seedy bingo hall. I had forgotten that the provinces were still crawling with dullards still labouring under a 1950s infatuation.' It was a puerile outburst that says more about the writer than the people who gathered happily on that television set.

Such pleasantries would soon be swept aside though, as Dawson's health and private life once again started to imitate that Pleasure Beach roller-coaster. A heart attack in London marked his card. This time, the warning came, not as a worrying judder, but one almighty slap. The drink, the cigarettes, the work, the worry, were all taking their effect.

When You're Smiling

It wasn't a question of slowing down; it was a question of stopping. Once past the Christmas Les spent hospitalised in 1991, he had to put financial worries aside and relax into the sedate pace of Lytham St Annes, where the average age is rumoured to be 86 and grey hair is considered a sign of delayed puberty.

> Les Dawson: 'As time passed by, I started to love and pine for my home life more and more. The simple things, back there at Lytham, slowly became far more important than anything showbusiness really had to offer. I started working in order only to keep that home life intact. The balance had shifted. It really had.'

> And this from *No Tears For The Clown*: 'The yawning sandy beaches of St Annes-on-Sea, the wide roads and clean air, the lovely vulgar mistress that is Blackpool, always beckoning with a saucy finger to the thrills she can offer, home at last.'

In those words one strongly senses a man who had finally realised where his own nirvana lay. Unlikely as it may seem, for Les Dawson it lay in Lytham St Annes – to each his own. And the happiness that lured him from his physical pain would soon be enhanced beyond belief by the very public news that Tracy was expecting a baby.

The news came as a surprise. Perhaps in the shadow of Les's illness, Tracy's natural radiance was understandably dimmed. It seemed to be a downward spiral, with Tracy nursing Les back to health, while suffering herself. They had both started to worry, and the worry was instantly wiped away on hearing the news.

Strangely, as this news began to filter out via the tabloids, an unlikely period of truce between the Dawsons and the press ensued. The expected reaction never happened. All the articles seemed upbeat, lively, hugely supportive. The papers, perhaps chastened by their readers' support for the couple, now saw no reason to attack. As cynical as this view may seem, the Dawsons' decision to broadcast their happiness on programmes such as *Good Morning With Anne And Nick* worked to superb effect. Les even backed away from the curmudgeonly mode he adopted after finally giving up smoking and, to a large extent, drinking.

He was to return to the drink, however, one memorable night at the opening of *Les Miserables* at Manchester's Palace Theatre. Dawson, in the audience, surrounded by the city's teeming showbiz and soccer stars, all quaffing champagne and posing like crazy for

A Wonderful Life

Another great dame performance in Dick Whittington

123

When You're Smiling

Les gets a BBC paycheque

A Wonderful Life

photographers from the *Manchester Evening News*, allowed his happiness to get the better of him. (Much to Tracy's dismay, it must be noted.)

It was a strange night, halted after the interval by a major technical hitch. As the crowd waited for the second half to begin, they were greeted by the sight of impresario Cameron Macintosh striding to the centre of the stage.

'I'm sorry,' he announced, 'But the performance cannot continue due to a technical fault in the machinery.'

The disappointment was immediately broken as Les Dawson leapt to his feet.

'In that case,' he shouted, 'can you tell us how it ends?'

It was a golden moment, quintessential Dawson and one that practically retrieved the evening from the brink of disappointment. In *No Tears For The Clown*, Dawson wrote that Macintosh was overwhelmed with gratitude – and invited Les to all of his openings.

Reality continued to bite, however, and the Dawsons moved to Christchurch while Les appeared in the Bournemouth stint for *Run For Your Wife*. It was a good season, too. Bournemouth suited Dawson, with its lazy, ageing grandeur, its defiantly reactionary air, its apparent indifference to trend or fad, heavily reminiscent of Lytham St Annes. For once, the play was effortlessly successful and, glowing with optimism, Les and Tracy would drive through the sunshine and haze of the New Forest and Purbeck, soaking in the surrounding beauty, dreaming of their future.

It soon came. On Saturday 3 October, 1992, Charlotte Emily Lesley Dawson was born, in Manchester, at St Mary's Hospital. The Dawsons' happiness would soon be shared with the rest of the British public, most entertainingly on *Good Morning With Anne And Nick*. Following their appearance, and to the delight of all concerned, the programme production room was flooded with congratulatory messages, letters, faxes, flowers and gifts. Even their old adversaries in the press continued their dubious support, sending bouquets to the Lytham house.

The beaming face of Les Dawson as he reached this state of bliss with his beautiful wife and daughter beside him is probably the best way to remember him. The final snapshot from a tumultuous life. He could have slowed down, perhaps. He could have slimmed and slowed and had a longer life, but that wouldn't have been Les. And Les, as Michael Parkinson noted, was Les. His untimely death in June 1993, from a heart attack while visiting hospital for a check-up, shouldn't be allowed to darken that wonderful, final happiness. He deserved it more than most.

When You're Smiling

Tracy: 'I don't think he could ever have given up. He talked about directing shows, producing shows and concentrating on his writing. And he was a very successful writer and it would have been nice if he could have been here today. But it didn't happen. Les lived life to the full and I think I'm right in saying that he had a wonderful life.'

Roy Barraclough: 'Every day, I think about Les. Something might happen and I think, "Oh God, Les would have loved that." And certainly now I am a great one for eavesdropping on conversations in cafes. On buses, when I hear two women talking I think, "That would have really suited Les and I".

*   *   *

Memories are made of this

Afterword

A celebratory air hangs over the city following Manchester United's treble-winning climax to the season. Few people would forget that hot Thursday night, when an estimated three-quarters of a million people danced on and around Deansgate, ushering the team's cup-laden bus down to a finale at the Manchester Evening News Arena. Three days later, with equal vigour, 50,000 Manchester City supporters would see their team claw their way past mighty Gillingham in the Second Division 'Play-Offs' at Wembley.

The optimism may be misplaced, but it has invaded every cafe bar, every themed pub, every art gallery, every night club. It infiltrates the city's now expansive Gay Village, it flows in the gossip of the office workers at the modernistic Salford Quays. What would Les Dawson make of such revelry? He would be bemused, one feels but, almost certainly... proud.

The buildings which towered above him, as a young boy, are still in place, though they are rather cleaner these days. Standing proud among them is Les Dawson's favourite building in the city, not because of its ornate exterior – it is rather bland to be honest – but for the warmth he found inside it. In August 1999, the Palace Theatre, his 'home' venue gained a welcome addition to its edifice. Showbiz charity Comic Heritage erected a blue plaque in honour of its favourite comedian... Les Dawson. (A Norman Evans plaque, coincidentally, will grace The Opera House.)

'I'm over the moon, Les was so proud of being a Mancunian,' Tracy Dawson told the *Manchester Evening News*. 'Not long before he died we drove around his native Collyhurst. I remember him crying because his home had gone. It had been pulled down. It upset him a lot, so a plaque in his memory at one of his favourite theatres would be wonderful.'

*   *   *

Picture Credits

BBC Enterprises p 85, 89, 107
Mirror Syndication p 8, 13, 20, 33, 81, 95, 99, 109
Pictorial Press p 7, 36, 124, 126
Rex Features p 11, 16, 35, 39, 90, 105, 112, 123
Scope Features p 15, 25, 26, 43, 44, 47, 48, 59, 65, 66, 75, 76, 78, 86, 102, 111
Scope Features/Allan Ballard p 73
Scope Features/Brian Moody p 83, 101
Yorkshire Television p 60

Pictures on p 11, 29, 49/50, 55, 63, 68, 82, 115, 116, 119 and 120
by kind permission of Tracy Dawson

The author and publishers have made every reasonable effort to contact all copyright holders. Any errors that may have occurred are inadvertent and anyone who for any reason has not been contacted is invited to write to the publishers so that a full acknowledgement may be made in subsequent editions of this work.

Bibliography

Les Dawson's Lancashire Les Dawson (*Elm Tree Books, 1983*)
A Clown Too Many, An Autobiography Les Dawson (*Hamish Hamilton 1985*)
No Tears For The Clown, An Autobiography Les Dawson (*Little, Brown 1992*)
Look Back With Laughter, Vol 2 Mike Craig (*Mike Craig 1998*)

Sources

Broadcasts: BBC Radio Four, *How Tickled I Am (1999)*; BBC Radio Four, *Start The Week* (1985); Manchester GMR Radio; Manchester Piccadilly Radio; Granada Television; Yorkshire Television

Newspapers: *Manchester Evening News; The Sunday Times, Daily Express, Daily Mirror, Blackpool Chronicle; Lancashire Evening Post; Yorkshire Post; Bury Times; Bury Press; Stockport Advertiser*